DIARY OF AN **ANGRY** PREGNANT WOMAN

The Emotion and Drama Behind one of the World's
Fastest, Most Controversial, and Unbelievable,
Postpartum Transformations

TRACI THOMAS

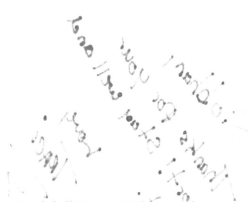

This book is intended for mature readers due to adult content and explicit language.
The author has tried to recreate events and conversations from her memory of
them. In order to maintain anonymity in some instances, the author has changed
the names of certain individuals and places, and also may have changed some
identifying characteristics and details such as physical properties, occupations and
places of residence.

The author of this book does not dispense medical advice or prescribe use of any
technique as treatment for physical, emotional, or medical conditions without the
advice of a medical professional/physician. The intent of the author is only to offer
information to help guide you on your quest for physical and emotional well-
being. In the event that you use any of the information in this book, which is your
constitutional right, the author assumes no responsibility for your actions.

ISBN: 0692314024
ISBN 13: 9780692314029
Library of Congress Control Number: 2014918656
1. Body After Baby   2. Post Pregnancy Weight
3. Postpartum Depression   4. Postpartum Fitness   5. Books About Affairs

Bombshell Xtreme, LLC
Orangeburg, South Carolina
BombshellXtreme.com

DEDICATION

For my son, Michael and my husband Curt, because without you, I wouldn't be where I am today. I was selfish and only thought of myself in everything I used to do and now I have become a totally different person. I am now living my life with a purpose. Thank you for coming into my life and making me into a better woman and a loving mother.

For Momma Bombshell, you are the True Queen of Fitness and foundation from where I've grown. Thank you for the opportunity you gave me and seeing the potential in me from the very beginning when we were both starting out. I told you my vision and everything happens for a reason. We both had to go through some things but regardless, I did tell you that I'd make you a proud Momma and I hope to work with you again in the near future, but in the pageant fitness world this time.

I'd also like to dedicate this book to all the broken hearted women who have ever felt pain from a man or someone they love. As a trainer to women, I take on the many emotions of my clients as they go through different cycles and changes in their lives. They entrust me with their innermost secrets and the problems they face daily. We all go through different trials in life and I am very non-judgmental. I love being there to help them channel their energy because I've been there myself. Just know that time heals all wounds and what doesn't kill you only makes you stronger. Embrace any setbacks and above all, stay positive.

With Love,
Traci

"People who consider themselves victims of their circumstances will always remain victims unless they develop a greater vision for their lives."

—Stedman Graham

CONTENTS

DIARY OF AN **ANGRY**
PREGNANT WOMAN

INTRODUCTION

52 lb weight gain

Aug 2012   Oct 2012
8 weeks after giving birth

See this picture here? You've probably seen it before somewhere on social media. This is a *real* transformation that *really* happened. My name is Traci Thomas, and I gained over sixty pounds during my pregnancy. I completely lost the weight within four weeks and then got totally ripped up in eight short weeks postpartum. Yes, there are thousands, maybe even hundred thousands, of women around the world (especially celebrities & fitness models) who have had amazing postpartum comebacks. Many of these women who do have extremely fast transformations didn't have the same type of massive weight gain I had; many of them just lost their baby bumps and didn't have much else to lose besides that. They're blessed with great genetics! Me? Not so much. I am not naturally thin, I have an athletic body but I'm on the thicker and solid side naturally. I have to work very hard day in and day out to stay in my "ideal" shape. The thing that separates me from these amazing women is the massive amount I gained, the speed in which I lost it, and also the severe and unsafe measures I took to do so. Doctors say that a healthy pregnancy weight gain for the average woman is twenty-five to thirty-five pounds; if you're an overweight woman it should only be fifteen to twenty-five pounds; if a woman is underweight, she should gain between twenty-eight to forty pounds to sustain a healthy pregnancy. Well, I gained a whopping sixty-one pounds even though I was super fit pre-pregnancy with a low body fat percentage. I even ate a clean vegan/vegetarian diet while pregnant and worked out one to three hours per day all the way up until my delivery date. If there are women who did gain over sixty pounds, then my guess is that their recovery time back to being fit and seeing lots of muscle tone and abs was likely not as fast as me. Why do I make this claim? Because no woman in her right mind, would put her body through what I did. I pushed my body dangerously to the maximum *XTREME* and started workouts immediately the same day of my delivery.

You see, I got my body fat down to fifteen percent and got totally ripped up within eight weeks after being over two hundred pounds, and that is unheard of. I actually considered contacting the *Guinness Book of World Records* to see if I could make it in for fast weight loss after a heavy pregnancy weight because what I did was borderline insanity! I was totally out of my mind and driven by my emotions. No, I didn't wait the recommended six weeks that doctors suggest for healing, and no, I wouldn't recommend that other new moms do the same thing, because it was a very dangerous and high risk thing for me to put my body through. You see, I look happy in the above picture, but what you don't know is what lies underneath that smile is a very angry (and slightly insane), bitter woman. Why was I angry? Well, that is what I will reveal to you in my diary. I was fed up with the way my life was going and there was a lot of emotion and mental toughness behind this transformation. My adrenaline and rage numbed me, so I felt no pain. Regardless of the circumstances that led to this crazy transformation, I am very thankful for the experience I had, and I have been blessed beyond belief from it.

This diary is adult oriented and does contain sexual content and explicit language in some of the chapters. I know I'm taking a huge blow to my character for writing this book, but its life and these are real life things that do happen; not everyone you see is as innocent as they may seem on the surface. Please try not to judge me too much for what I'm about to reveal about my life. Though I'm now a happily married mother and part of the Pageant Industry as a judge and personal trainer to young beauty queens, I am by no means perfect; I was never fit to be in a running for Miss America or Miss Universe because I don't have the squeaky clean past required to be fit for a crown or title. I have many skeletons in my closet that date back to when I was a teenager growing up in New York. The life that I have lived thus far has been tailored to fit me and only me and everything I've been through was necessary to give me life experiences so that I may help other women and young ladies who may be facing similar struggles I had. I love to keep young girls focused on their goals. I feel as if I'm living out my dreams vicariously through these gifted and beautiful young ladies by helping to cultivate them into something I never thought I could be.

Honestly, I could write another book about my teenage years because I know it would help a lot of other young girls dealing with balancing academics, sports, social life, boys/relationships, eating disorders, bullying, mental illness, and body image issues (yes I experienced all those) that I have overcome later in my life. You name it, I've been through it at such a young age. Looking at where I am today, you'd never guess the type of childhood I had. I came from a great family but I was a very difficult and manipulative child who believed that good grades gave me the green light to do whatever I wanted to. I grew up pretty fast in New York clubbing (I had a fake ID), dating celebrities, and professional athletes all before I was eighteen years old. It took something tragic to stop me on my destructive path. Though I was an honor student, I put my parents through hell with my social life. Actually, this subject will be my next memoir, a self-help with proper content for teen girls about my teenage years. I've been through things that could have caused my demise but through prayer and grace, I'm still alive and able to share my experience with other women and young ladies.

I don't want to reveal too much about my next book but the events that occurred in my past, led me into the workforce as a bartender/waitress; where the first chapter of this diary begins. The subsequent book coming out later will definitely shine a light on how I got to this point in my life and also explain the psychology behind it. This diary that you're about to read is the climax and pivotal point in my life where everything has changed for the better; things turned bad for me before they turned good. This is the story from only the last seven years of my life summed up into nineteen chapters. I am sharing it to clear up all the negativity and doubt from the skeptics about what I've done in my controversial transformation picture. It's a great relief to let out what I've been holding inside about what I really went through during this delicate and challenging time. I accumulated lots of great information from different sources during my pregnancy and all that I learned can be found in this book in the last few chapters. Hopefully this will be able to help other women out there having questions about pregnancy and fitness and also be able to help women channel their emotions and anger. Would I be able to do this transformation all over again with a second pregnancy? My answer would be yes, but more than likely it would not be nearly as fast because I am not that ANGRY woman anymore.

Bombshell Xtreme Fitness Story

IT'S NO LONGER A SECRET

YOU'RE INVITED

CHAPTER 1

MR. FAMOUS
BODYBUILDER

1

Dear Diary,

I was having a regular Friday morning bar shift at the restaurant known for its buxom, beautiful servers and hot wings. As usual, the day started off pretty slowly. When I worked the morning bar shift, I got a lot of cleaning done and pretty much got everything prepped and ready for the night bartender. I had a few daily morning regulars who came to see me, but on this day in particular, it was very slow. As I was restocking beer in the cooler and replacing to-go cups and utensils, I noticed a black SUV with tinted windows pulling into the parking lot with some type of nutritional supplement advertisement wrapped all around it. Out stepped two really attractive Caucasian gentlemen. One looked to be Italian, he was tall, dark, and handsome (in the mid-thirties range), and the other was much younger (early twenties) and a bit shorter but built like a Greek god; he looked phenomenal! He had on a red tank top with yellow lettering that read 'BSN Finish First' across his massive chest and his muscles were popping out all over the place. He had an extremely small waistline compared to the rest of him. His skin was flawless and his hair was cut very low and neat with long shaped up sideburns. This dude was incredibly handsome.

Naturally, I was physically attracted to him because I love fitness and fit people, plus he captivated everyone's attention when he walked in. These two men came in and sat in another section of the restaurant, away from the bar. Their server happened to be in the back break room, probably on her cell phone, so I didn't hesitate to walk over to them and immediately began service taking their drink orders. Since the restaurant was so slow at that time, I walked to the break room and asked the girl, who was supposed to be their waitress, if I could go ahead and serve them and invite them to relocate to the bar. She said no and that she'd be right out to serve them. It was pretty slow so I guess she really wanted the tip. I let her know I already ran their drinks and that they were ready to order their food. I then went back to the bar and kept catching eye contact with Mr. Muscleman anyway. He seemed to be attracted to me as well.

After the gentlemen got their food, I walked back over to their table and asked, "Hey what do you do? You have quite a serious look going on there. Are you famous or something? A model or a wrestler? We get all types of famous people to come through here all the time."

He said, "I'm a bodybuilder, and I'm here on business making appearances."

I said, "Shut up! No, you aren't. So you're famous for real?"

He laughed and said, "I guess I have become pretty well known in the fitness industry. This is my manager," he said, gesturing to the tall, dark, and handsome Italian guy who was licking the wing sauce off his fingers.

His manager then said, "You've probably seen him before if you read any fitness magazines. He's featured in stories and ads in just about every printed magazine out right now. Google him, he's being considered the future of bodybuilding and only 21 years old."

I told him that if it was true, then it was very cool and that I was also into fitness. I told him that I didn't know much about bodybuilding but that I taught aerobics classes several times a week.

"Did you happen to see that big Gold's Gym at the next exit up?" He shook his head saying yes while he had a mouthful of food. "Well that's where I go when I get off from here and I teach aerobics classes. I have three hours left before I can leave! Looking at you makes me want to bust into a squat right now! Haha!"

He said, "Haha that's cool. You actually remind me of my teammate, Alicia Marie. She's a very stunning and beautiful woman, just about as tall as you are, with the same long and lean build as you. You should probably consider becoming a fitness competitor or model. You'd probably do really well because you have an awesome exotic and Amazon look for the fitness stage. You're a tall glass, exactly how tall are you? Those legs look longer than yard sticks!"

Blushing, I said, "Thank you, I'm six feet tall, they call me the Six Foot Bombshell here."

"Dang girl! You should really think about fitness modeling and competing. Check this out."

He then wiped the hot wing sauce off his hands onto a wet napkin and reached for his phone to do a Google image search of his colleague to show me who she was.

I said, "Wow! What do you know about the T-Mobile SideKick? I have the same one as you in white! Haha!"

"Yeah it's a pretty cool phone, my manager got this one for me exclusively for business and he screens my texts and calls but I'm more of a Blackberry user." He began to search through the browser then handed his phone to me. I immediately saw the similarities. We had the same facial structure and similar features but she had a slightly darker skin complexion than me. She was so very strikingly beautiful. Don't get me wrong, I was pretty confident that I had a great physique with nice, long, toned, track-runner legs and an awesome six-pack, but Alicia Marie's body was sheer PERFECTION! She was way more lean and conditioned than me with rips and muscle tone all over, not one ounce of fat on her. She had the body of a *Fitness Goddess* with perfect symmetry from head to toe! I was so inspired by her beauty and her flawless physique. I told him that I'd love to look that amazing and his manager told me that I could definitely look like her with the right type of training and nutrition. I smiled and began to imagine my life being a famous fitness model like Alicia Marie. Mr. Bodybuilder, also showed me pictures of ads he was featured in and he did seem to be a big deal in the industry, I was very impressed because I had him beat in age by two years and he was very focused for his young age. Here I was, working in this restaurant trying to figure out my next move in life and this young man seemed to be really have it together, focused and knew exactly what he wanted out of life already.

The crowd began to pick up in the restaurant, and I had to go back behind the bar to serve my customers. It was almost time for shift change and also happy hour. I handed him back his phone and I told him that I wished him well in everything he was doing and that I had to get back to work. I left to go take care of my new customers who just walked in. I was hoping for him to ask me for my number before I walked away but he didn't.

On his way out, he walked up to the bar to slip me a twenty-dollar tip, even though I wasn't his server (I loved working in a fun restaurant where we always got above-average tips). He said," I'll see you around. It was nice meeting you babygirl." I was very appreciative but also very sad that he didn't give me his number or ask for mine. I wasn't going to ask for his information because I never approached guys in that way. I gave all the hints and body gestures that I was really interested in him, but as handsome and good as he looked, he probably had a girlfriend already. A man that good looking, who's a famous fitness model can't be single. He walked out never to be seen again.

After the bar was stocked up and ready to go, I closed out my last bar tab, counted my cash drawer down, took my tips out, and then had the day manager transfer a couple tabs over to the night bartender to clock me out. It was time for my second gig, teaching aerobics, which was my passion. My manager, who happened to be female, took my spin classes sometimes. My nickname for her was Master P. We had a cool employee/boss relationship; we were both Virgos two years and two days apart in age (me Sept 2 and her Sept 4, she was older). She was so pretty with a caramel/tan skin complexion and wore her real hair long and brownish blonde like Beyoncé. When I found out she was a Virgo we really hit it off. In the restaurant, she ruled and was my boss, but in the gym, I was her boss and told her what to do; she'd always come up with excuses to miss my class.

As she clocked me out she said, "Save me a bike in the back row!"

"No, I'll save you one in the front row right in front of the stage so I can push you harder to make sure you don't cheat yourself out of a good workout."

"Um that's ok! I probably won't make it anyway, its biker's night and Antwan needs my help with something so it looks like I'll be here for at least another hour or so helping him."

"Right! You better still come anyway, do some cardio and work on your abs, no excuses girl!"

While giving me two thumbs up she said, "Sure will!"

We both walked away laughing knowing good and well that she wasn't going to come train that night. She wasn't like the typical manager we were used to. Master P, was a pretty hot chick, when she got interviewed to be hired; we thought she was applying to work amongst us and not above us. P, was in pretty great shape with a tight curvy physique, but I told her not to settle and that she could be way tighter than she was and look bikini ready all the time. Her attitude was that she didn't have to look picture perfect to fit into an extra small uniform like us. She was our manager, and I doubt she'd be able to participate in our bikini contests because of her corporate position, but she was pretty hot enough to make the annual swimsuit calendar if she were working as a bartender or waitress. She typically worked out in spurts, one week she'd do really well coming to the gym, eating healthy seafood and salads from the menu; then the next she'd fall off completely by eating fried buffalo shrimp with blue cheese dip and french fries saying, "Screw it! I don't have to be fit, y'all do! I'm enjoying my food!"

"But P, you're not going to stay young forever. Once you hit thirty it'll start to show. Trust me, I know too many women playing catch-up at the gym now who got comfortable because they had a great metabolism while they were young. We are far from thirty but it'll be easier to maintain instead of waiting for it to happen!" She was very humorous about her fitness but I tried to keep her motivated despite her being comfortable with her physique.

After I was done chatting with Master P, I grabbed my bag from my cubby in the break room and went into the bathroom to change out of my uniform. I put on my gym attire, tied my hair into a high ponytail, and then headed to the gym. As I was driving through traffic, I had my spin music up loud and going over my new choreography in my head. At Gold's, it was very hard to get on the schedule to teach because all the instructors were very competitive and really good. You had to know your choreography perfectly without making any mistakes because they'd watch you as a "ghost member", making sure you give the right cues at the right time of the right beat of the music. This type of practice kept us all very sharp and experts at our chosen craft. You'd get snatched off the schedule in a heartbeat and get replaced with someone else more proficient if you couldn't keep up with the current releases of choreography. As I was pulling up into the gym parking lot, my focus was broken when I noticed the same black SUV that had come to the restaurant earlier was parked smack in front of the gym illegally. I gasped; my heart began to beat fast as I quickly looked for a space to park so I could hurry inside.

I could feel sweat begin to roll down my back as my adrenaline already began to pump. I walked through the doors and quickly made my way past the daycare and front desk. I peeked through the large crowd of people to see that all the fuss was over my handsome bodybuilder friend from earlier, and he was signing autographed pictures and being photographed with gym members and staff. There was also a huge banner picture of him in the background that read, *The Phenom*. My jaw nearly dropped because I didn't expect to see him again. He smiled when he saw me, and I walked over to him with my arms folded smiling as well. I asked him why he didn't tell me he was doing his appearance at my gym, because I did recall telling him that I worked at the Gold's up the street during our conversation. He said that when I told him where I'd be headed after work, he knew that he would see me again and wanted to talk to me outside of the restaurant/bar environment. He figured many other guys probably tried to hit on me while working there, so he'd rather talk to me at the gym. I asked him how much longer he would be signing autographs, and he said a couple more hours. I told him I would be right back after my class, and I ran upstairs to the cardio deck and the spin room where I taught RPM (spinning).

It felt like an eternity went by while I was teaching because I was so unfocused and anxious to get back downstairs to where he was. When I finished teaching, I asked the next instructor coming in to answer any questions anyone had and told my class I had somewhere to be and had to leave out quickly. I totally neglected my students by rushing out; it was so out of character because I usually engage and interacted with my class pretty well, but I wanted to get back to the sexy Mr. Phenom. I was overly excited and I hurried back down to the first floor. We exchanged contact information, then I found out he would be in town for a couple more days to make appearances at other gyms.

I couldn't wait to get to know Mr. Bodybuilder. We hung out the next night, and I brought my co-worker, Jamz, from the restaurant with me just in case he was a little crazy. He showed up with his manager, so maybe he was thinking the same thing about me too; touché, it evened things out. We met at a local restaurant called Copper River, which served us some amazing pizza and drinks. We got along so well, like we were best friends who had known each other for a very long time, and the attraction was crazy. He had a very nice swagger, and I could tell he liked black chicks. I also found out that he was a Leo, which greatly explained his cockiness and arrogance. I'm a Virgo, so we actually were very compatible according to the stars. I found out that he lived in Atlanta and that was almost a four-hour drive down I-20 from South Carolina.

After we hit it off, we both took frequent trips back and forth to spend time with each other, and I became his girlfriend. I was so happy, and I loved how much he taught me about weight -lift training, nutrition, and bodybuilding. I loved going to the gym to watch him lift while I did cardio, and he turned me on to a whole new side of fitness that eventually became an addiction and passion to me!

We began to have a very intimate relationship, and I could see an amazing future with him as a fitness power couple. The attention that we got while we were out was intense! People couldn't help but stare at us because of his massive build and my tall fitness model-like looks and not to mention our choco-caramel/vanilla swirl! He was so young and everyone was so amazed at his phenomenal physique at his age. We were such a sight to see and I felt so lucky to be on his arm, especially when his fans would approach us for his autograph and sometimes mine too thinking I was Alicia Marie! It was surreal.

I had never been with a white man sexually before, and he was way more than I expected! I've always heard rumors that white guys were pretty small, especially bodybuilders, but this wasn't true at all! He was well-endowed and he treated me like his ebony queen! Physically, he had a hard and intimidating exterior, but he loved to cuddle and showed me so much affection. I fell in love with him and began to picture what our children would look like, being mixed and having such great athletic genetics from both parents. We even spoke about how our kids would be beautiful, super genetic freaks! After a few months went by, I told him I was thinking about transferring to the same restaurant chain in Atlanta and wanted to work at his gym as a pump and spin instructor. I also told him that I was ready to begin training to compete in a fitness show to pursue a Pro Card and Sponsorship Deal. I wanted him to be my mentor by showing me the ropes of getting started in the fitness industry. Soon after I told him this, he took me to meet his parents and also his other manager and trainer, who lived in Georgia, to discuss prepping me for my first show.

When I met his parents, I was afraid they wouldn't be too accepting of me because racism is still alive here in the south and I wasn't white, but to my surprise they were extremely nice and accepting. His mother showed awesome southern hospitality and offered me lemonade and snacks. I was very uptight and shy at first and I guess Mr. Bodybuilder's dad could tell how nervous I was to meet them, so he told jokes to make us all laugh to help me feel a bit more comfortable. I could see where Mr. Phenom got his athletic physique because his mom was pretty fit for her age and his dad's body, especially his legs, looked pretty well built up. I could already imagine his folks being pretty cool and down to earth in-laws. I really adored them! They seemed to like me a lot and appeared to be happy that we were together as a couple. After chatting with his parents, he then took me to a supplement nutrition store in downtown Atlanta, where he worked part time, to meet with his other manager/trainer who helped him with his show prep.

When I met his manager, he appeared pretty cool at first and I was excited to begin working with him, but then he kind of rubbed me the wrong way when I heard him say something and I didn't trust him. I stepped out of his office to use the restroom and fix myself up (girl stuff) and upon returning I could overhear them both engaged in a conversation about me. His manager said, "Wow! She's so much prettier and seems much nicer than Crystal. Her boobs are smaller but surgery can fix that later. You've done well; she is definitely way hotter than Crystal!" (I'm going to use the name Crystal because I don't want to use certain names in this book to protect identities). They got quiet when I walked back into the office to sit down.

"Wow! So this is the Six Foot Bombshell I've been hearing so much about. You've got legs for days! You are one tall girl and you're not even wearing heels! Well tell me a little about yourself. You've definitely come to the right place, you can kill in this industry. I was thinking I'd train you for Figure but you're so long and lean and your face is very striking, that jaw line! There's a new Bikini Division starting up and you will be perfect for it. Your look is very marketable; we can turn you into a star."

Mr. Bodybuilder said, "I'll leave you two to talk, I'm gon' go get my next meal in."

His manager said, "I've got some venison in there, you can help yourself to it."

"Oh word? Thanks! Good lookin' out bro."

Mr. Bodybuilder walked out the office to heat up his food and I was alone with his manager. He began asking about my goals and about how much he thought my contest stage weight should be, after he cut down my body fat percentage, for my height.

"I think 155 pounds is a good solid stage weight for you. Don't want you looking too skinny. You look like you're doing too much cardio. You're going to have to lift heavier because I want to bulk you a bit more to fill you out and cap your shoulders." My arms were folded as he spoke to me and everything he was saying went in one ear and out the other. I didn't want to add bulk and I didn't want a male trainer, especially one that I couldn't trust because he knew something and wasn't telling me. I had no interest in moving forward with him being my contest coach, I was ready to leave so that I could interrogate Mr. Bodybuilder about the conversation they had before I walked in. I sat there thinking to myself,

Who the fuck is Crystal? Why hasn't he mentioned her to me? Well, after we left the nutrition shop and were on our way to the gym, I told Mr. Bodybuilder that I overheard the conversation they had and asked him who she was. After beating around the bush, I finally got the truth out of him. Crystal was his other girlfriend, who lived in Staten Island and worked for the company he was endorsed to. He told me that their relationship was fairly new, like ours, and that he met us both around the same time, just a few weeks apart. She lived far away up north and he liked what he saw when he met me. He said he liked both of us and wanted to see which of us he liked better and wanted to be with.

He was two timing me but at least he was being honest with me and didn't lie about it; when he told me this, I was completely heartbroken! I saw a great future with him, following in his same footsteps to become a famous fitness model. He was my inspiration, and I placed him high on a pedestal, but those dreams of having a future with him were crushed. I never allow myself to be somebody's second option or choice! He was two years younger than me and probably wasn't ready to settle down with one woman. I told him that I'd make the choice for him, and I walked away from the relationship. It was very hard to do because I really loved him, but I had to protect my heart from being hurt any more than it already was. I never had to compete for a man, and I wasn't going to give him that much power over me. I had him to bring me back to his place so that I could pack my things and leave never to return again. I cried almost the entire drive back to South Carolina. I called out sick from the restaurant and found substitutes to teach my gym classes for an entire week, love can really make you feel physically sick; I had no desire to be around people. I just wanted to stay in bed and couldn't interact with anyone, let alone having to motivate people to work out and be gleefully smiling all day. I ripped up his autographed photo and magazines he was featured in and threw them into my parent's fireplace to burn. I stopped accepting his calls and cut off all forms of communication with him. I removed him from my number-one friend spot on my Myspace page and deleted him from my life.

It was tough trying to erase him from my mind completely because he was the one who started me on a new fitness journey as an amateur fitness bikini competitor. He was the inspiration that led me to become a nationally qualified athlete. I was South Carolina State's first Bikini Fitness Tall-Class Champion and Overall winner for the first year the NPC Bikini Division began. I ran into him frequently at different national-level shows, but he didn't look like the same guy I had fallen in love with. When I saw him on the stage, he didn't look as lean, cut, and conditioned as he was when we were together; he seemed to have lost his focus and I could feel his energy that he was stressed out over something. I'm not sure of what it was because I never asked nor did I want to intrude in on his relationship with Crystal; in my mind, I'd like to believe it was her who was causing him unnecessary stress.

This Crystal seemed like a handful. I didn't know her personally, but she'd inbox my Myspace account with the drama they had going on. She asked me questions about things like clothing I had apparently forgotten to pack and left behind at Mr. Bodybuilder's house months after our breakup. I never responded to her but I texted Mr. Bodybuilder to tell his girlfriend not to contact me with their problems because I didn't want to partake in their drama. When I found out who she was, I just had to see if she looked better than me (Most girls do this to see if their ex upgraded or downgraded). I checked her Myspace out and judging from her photos, she was a very pretty Italian looking girl. She was super fit with six pack abs and had an exotic look just like myself except she was white. She had long pretty brunette hair like Kim Kardashian, greyish-blue eyes with heavy dark eyeliner, and huge fake tits that always seemed to be pushed way up to her neck in all her photos. Just like Mr. Famous Bodybuilder, I saw on her page that she too was a Leo. I could see why he was attracted to her physically because she was a pretty hot chick but this girl seemed to be super high maintenance though, and also very stressful to deal with; if that's what he wanted then that's what he got. Two fiery Leos together was probably a terrible match anyway because Leos are usually bossy; there was probably a power struggle and they'd more than likely argue and fight a lot.

I later heard that Mr. Famous Bodybuilder got released from his big contract with the company who sponsored him and then stopped competing. I really want to believe that his relationship with Crystal could have been one of the reasons why he never turned pro as a bodybuilder; she wasn't the right positive energy he needed to bring out the best in him. He was physically attracted to her but probably couldn't connect any deeper than that physical aspect of their relationship. I really felt bad for him and wanted to reach out but then remembered the heartache and pain he'd brought into my life and decided to just move on. I'm sure that if I never found out about her that he would have never told me and would play both of us since we all lived in different states. I believed losing his contract and leaving the industry was his karma for hurting me. The woman he ended up with brought him down. I kept moving on with the knowledge and inspiration he instilled in me, despite his downfall. Every time I step onto a fitness stage, I remember where it all started from and can never forget Mr. Famous Bodybuilder.

After placing in the top ten at my first national-level show in Vegas (the first year of the NPC Bikini Division), I joined forces with one of the world's biggest and best training teams for women's Figure and Bikini Fitness, Team Bombshell. The name allured me and the girls on the team really stood out wearing uniformed black velour suits with their names and they all had on the same type of smoked eyed makeup. They really stood out on the stage from the other competitors too. They were called Bombshells and their hair, skin, and nails looked so amazing and healthy; they didn't look skinny, dried out, or dehydrated; they were ripped up yet very feminine and curvy with some incredibly small waistlines; smaller than all the other competitors and it looked so unrealistic! They looked like fit Barbie dolls. Typically you'd expect that gorgeous women like these would be very stuck up, competitive, and mean, but their energy was so amazing and it was like a sorority sisterhood of fitness and beauty, they were very inviting into their circle. I wanted to have the same Fitness Barbie Doll look these girls had and be part of them; plus I already coined the name SixFootBombshell at work so it seemed very fitting for me to join a training team with a similar name.

I really hit it off with the founder of this team quickly; when I met her at my first Bombshell Bootcamp, she became my gym momma and hired me to be her personal assistant and group fitness manager at her fitness center. She reigned over us all and we called her Momma Bombshell. She too was a Leo, and I learned all her fitness secrets and tricks to staying hydrated and nourished to look great on the stage and how to attain a super tiny waistline for the signature Bombshell bikini fitness "stage look." Her training was the most intense training I had ever experienced, I thought I was in pretty good shape already but it really kicked my butt! The meal planning was amazing and tasted so good. She was truly gifted at her craft and knew how to transform any type of body into a bikini or figure champion physique.

Our team was known (Still current) for having the most beautifully shaped women with unbelievable small waistlines. A large number of professional competitors and celebrities were birthed from this team and the majority of women seen in fitness magazines who grace the covers, even still today, come from this prodigious team of athletes as well. At one point there was almost an entire saturation of Bombshells doing NPC shows and we really dominated the field. Other teams have been founded over the years (many of the girls branched out and started their own training and teams) and all our fitness and beauty secrets got leaked out to the masses; regardless of our secrets being leaked, Team Bombshell ruled the fitness industry, the most successful in turning out the most Pro athletes before other teams were established. I lost touch with my gym momma over the years because my personal drama hindered my training and ability to work with her; the knowledge I gained from her about supplements, nutrition, staying hydrated, and how to achieve a small waistline is what ultimately helped me with my fast postpartum transformation.

None of this would have ever happened if I'd never met Mr. Famous Bodybuilder—who broke my heart. I don't know where he is now, but he was a great blessing to me, despite causing me pain. I'd like to thank him for inviting me into his world, starting me on my journey, and changing my life's path completely. When I met him, I was a college dropout just working and trying to figure out my life; I'm not sure which direction I was headed if we'd never met but he led me to my gym Momma. The fitness industry has become my passion and I gained a world of knowledge being part of such an amazing team of Bombshell coaches and athletes. Everyone we encounter in life serves as a purpose and learning experience to lead us to our destiny. My passion for fitness continued as I chased my dreams of becoming a bikini fitness pro and landing a nice endorsement, like my ex, Mr. Phenom, The Famous Bodybuilder.

Moving on and staying strong.
Yours Truly,
Traci

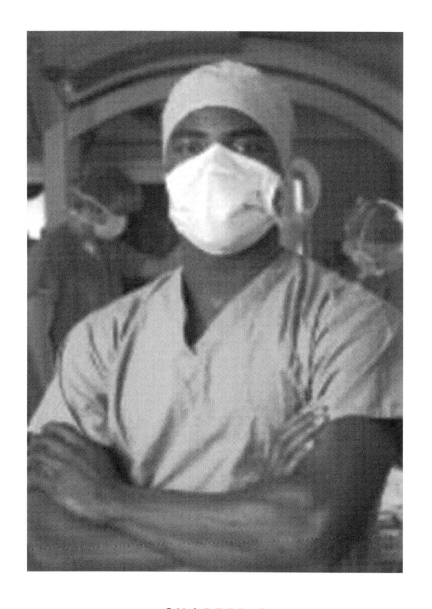

CHAPTER 2

MR. ER DOCTOR

Dear Diary,

I couldn't stay out sick from work too long because when you work for tips, any days off can affect your income greatly so my daily hustle resumed at the restaurant. I came back more determined than ever to succeed and become a sponsored athlete after such a heart-wrenching breakup. I wanted Mr. Famous Bodybuilder to see me doing well in his industry without him. I began saving money for shows and after meeting my gym Momma, I began to work as many extra shifts as I could to be able to afford my relocation to take the position with Team Bombshell in Florida. I also needed to be able to pay for my traveling expenses, swim-suits for my competitions, and a few months of rent money upfront, to room in a beach house with a couple of the Bombshells. I picked up floor shifts and bar shifts and started working doubles (12- 14 hour days).

One day, I picked up a Thursday night bar shift and I got to our Jumpstart early. Jumpstart was a meeting all the Girls had with the man-ager before beginning our shift. At Jumpstart, the manager made sure we looked camera ready with no gum in our mouth, no visible tattoos or piercings (flawless hair, make-up, nails), and had on perfect fitting uniforms (no runs in our tights, no scrunches or folds in our shorts, and no stains on our sketchers). We were informed about what specials were currently running, what beers and mixed drinks to push, and also what menu items we needed to sell to the customers. On this one night in particular, one of the pretty day-shift girls, Anita aka Pocahontas, came over to me as I was counting my cash drawer.

She said, "You see that guy sitting over there in my section? He wanted me to ask you to come to over to say hi to him. I think he thinks you're hot!"

I looked over at him and then rolled my eyes and continued to count my cash drawer. I said, "Girl, I'm not even clocked in and I'm not ready to talk to anyone yet. Tell him I'm busy, plus I'm on bar and not working the floor tonight." I was so not looking for another heartbreak; I just wanted to focus on myself. This man happened to be older, in his late thirties or early forties.

After our shift jumpstart meeting was over, I walked up to the bar to make sure everything was in order for the night. The ice on the beer was melted down and just needed to get covered with a little more. I walked to the back to scoop some ice from the machine and carried two buckets back to cover the beer. While dumping the bucket, I heard a man call my name from the front of the bar (we had a very large bar that could seat more than twenty people).

"Hey Traci... Six Foot Bombshell. That's your name right?"

I glanced over my shoulder and noticed that it was the same gentleman who wanted me to come speak to him earlier. Anita, must've given him my name. I still wasn't ready to talk so I ignored him, acting as if he wasn't there. I was wishing he'd go back to bug his waitress because she was a really pretty Indian girl who was a Pre-Med major just working to make extra money while in school. She had way more going for herself than me so I wondered why he was bothering me instead of her. I did a little bit more inspecting of the bar and took my sweet time, knowing I had to say something to him eventually because I was clocked in and it was my job to be bubbly like a cheerleader, happy-go-lucky, always smile, and stick to our "12 Steps of Hospitality" giving a great experience.

"One moment please sir, let me get settled." Once I was done inspecting the bar, I smiled and said, "Yes sir, how may I help you?" He asked me for an O'Doul's beer and then grabbed a bar stool and sat down. I slipped him a coaster and sat the open beer with a frosted mug in front of him.

He pushed the chilled glass back to me, took a sip from his bottle and said, "I don't need the mug, I like to drink from the bottle. So, are you a college student?"

"Yes, but I took the semester off to work, I kept changing my major and was wasting money."

"Well what do you study? What interests you?"

"I started with biology because I love science but it was too hard to keep up with all my labs due to being on the road with basketball, track, and cross-country. Then I changed to psychology, and then changed schools and switched to sport management with a minor in Spanish. Until I figure out exactly what I want to do I'm taking time off to work; I may just finish online. You've got a very nice accent. Are you Jamaican?"

"No, I'm from Nassau, maybe I'll get to take you there one day."

"That's the Bahamas right?"

"Correct. So you're an athlete. That explains your athletic body, with legs like those you look like you could outrun a gazelle! Let me guess, a hurdler?"

I laughed and said, "I am pretty quick and no, I actually hate hurdles. I'm a mid-distance runner; I do the mile, 800, and 400 meters. Would you like to order anything else, sir?"

"No, I already ate and I just came up for some conversation."

I placed his tab in a rocks glass in front of him and said, "Well I'll be back to check on you in a few."

He reminded me of the British actor, Idris Elba, from the TV series, *The Wire*. I do admit that he was very attractive to me, although he appeared to be nearly fifteen years my senior. He stood about six foot four or five and had a smooth, dark skin complexion; an athletic build; broad shoulders; big muscular arms; a small, fit waist; a nice chest; and very attractive salt-and-pepper hair. He was well groomed, like he took great care of himself and worked out regularly. Even his nails were clean and looked manicured and buffed. I stand six feet even, so his height was really appealing to me. He looked like he could lift me up easily with no trouble. I could wear my four- and five-inch heels with him with no worry of being taller than him. He even had a sexy Caribbean accent that was very pleasant to hear.

After our short exchange, I wasn't able to give him too much more attention because when I came onto the bar, it was already fairly busy. I had a few tabs that were being transferred over to me, and I had to tend to them to make sure they were OK. There were a bunch of drink tickets that had to be made for the girls working the floor and to-go orders that needed to be taken care of. The phone was ringing off the hook; it was chaotic, he could see how busy I was and that I didn't have much time to entertain his conversation. When I turned back to check on him after tending to the other patrons' orders, he had gone but he left a ten-dollar bill with a few singles and his business card inside the rocks glass. I looked at his card, and it said he was a physician; titles never impressed me. I didn't keep up with his card, and I may have trashed it by mistake with some old receipts when I cashed out his tab. I wasn't really interested in contacting him anyway.

A week went by, and I got a message that a Dr. Edward Grey had called and left a message for me. He left his number for me to reach him, but I still didn't call. Then the following week, he came back to the restaurant while I wasn't there, and the girl who was waitressing the tables in the bar area served him. I guess the girl who served him was attracted to him, because I was told by the day shift bartender that they spoke for a very long time and that she was bragging about getting a number from a cute doctor. When I found this out and also found out who the girl was, I couldn't stop thinking about him. I started to have thoughts like, *What if he's a really good guy? I mean, he's a doctor, for Christ's sake. He must have his shit together at his age and not looking for a fling or to just play games. He's older than my ex and probably ready to settle down.* He was going out of his way to get my attention, and I was being mean because of my recent heartbreak. I decided to go ahead and pursue him back. Another reason I pursued him was because I didn't like the girl who got his number. She was very pretty but one of those mean and stuck up I'm better than everyone else types and I didn't think she deserved to have him if he really was a good catch; it'd make her even more conceited to be dating a doctor.

I searched the restaurant caller ID for his number and gave him a call. We spoke for hours, and I found out that he was a traveling ER doctor who worked in my town from time to time. I also found out that his astrological sign was in Cancer, and I adored Cancers; they are really compatible with Virgos. I immediately began to think that this man would need nothing from me but love and companionship because he had an awesome career and money to burn. I have been burned for money from guys I've dated in the past, with the exception of Mr. Famous Bodybuilder, he had his own money.

Despite the fifteen year age gap between us, I found him to be very handsome and well put together, with a great sense of style. It felt like a dream because he treated me so well. He was such a gentleman; he opened doors for me and treated me like a lady. I never had to reach into my purse to pay for anything, and it wasn't long before I got the keys to his huge, amazing house (not sure why it was so big since it was just him living there), his cars, and his heart. The only rule he gave me for dating him was that I needed to own a passport because he traveled frequently abroad and wanted me to accompany him. I applied for one and had it expedited because he had a two week trip planned for us to tour Greece just weeks away.

Greece was so amazing! We had private car service almost everywhere in Athens, went shopping, visited different islands, rented four wheelers, swam in an underwater volcano, and ate in high end restaurants. He purchased a large, expensive, and exotic piece of art made out of crystals and mirrors and had it shipped back to the United States to put in his living room. People thought we were celebrities because he was so tall and looked like a retired NBA player leaving big tips for everyone, spending money like water, and I was tall and model-licious. So many people wanted to be photographed with us; we eventually played along and pretended he was a retired pro athlete; it was quite a funny experience and we had a ball with it. A woman even approached me to give me an Evil Eye Jeweled necklace, telling me to wear it for protection from evil stares from people who may look at me with envious eyes because of my beauty. It was an amazing journey with Dr. Grey. We explored the world first class together and he gave me all my first European experiences, I had never flown so much in one year! A girl could get used to this type of lifestyle, I was so in love and saw myself spending the rest my life with him.

He supported everything I was doing, and he loved the fact that I took care of my body, taught aerobics, ate healthy, and did fitness shows. I helped him to eat better while he worked and prepared his meals for him to take. He was an independent contracting doctor who charged a substantial amount for his services and he traveled all over to different parts of the world where he was licensed to work. Once while on vacation, he got called to fill in for a twenty-four hour shift and he charged the hospital almost double his fee and got seat upgrades for the flight because of the inconvenience being out of the country on vacation. They flew us back to the states first class and paid him a whopping seven hundred dollars per hour for twenty-four hours of work. Needless to say he made back the vacation money and then some.

When he worked nearby, I'd spend time with him on the clock and watched him work in the emergency room. I bet the nurses thought I was half crazy because I'd just be there with him for hours watching all the emergency room chaos; it was very entertaining. He was really busy but he'd find time to flirt with me without anyone seeing. I loved playing out my doctor/patient fantasy with him. He was the only black physician in most of the hospitals that he worked in and very well respected; I was so fascinated with his profession. He was the boss and all the nurses and staff had to do whatever he told them to do. I could tell the staff enjoyed working with him because he was so funny and always told jokes to keep them laughing; not to mention he was chocolate eye candy. There was never a dull moment, you never knew what type of emergency would come in and he was really great at getting patients in and out very quickly. Especially the ones labeled the "Frequent Flyers" who liked to make recurrent visits solely to get prescription drugs. He could always call out bullshit stories from people like that just trying to get a fix. He intrigued me so much and I admired him.

Over a year went by and I was spending more time in his home because he lived in a beautiful gated golf community just a few exits away from my job and the commute was shorter. I basically became his live-in girlfriend, and he sponsored a few of my shows, buying everything I needed; my expensive bikinis and my hair, makeup, and tanning. I actually lost focus with him because we were traveling so much and my training and diet got messed up. He expressed to me that he didn't want me to move away to take the assisting and management job with Team Bombshell in Florida, so he also paid for my training and travel expenses to continue working with the team as a member and I was living with him; I was neglecting my distance training. I'd never had this type of man before and was so used to paying for all my own expenses. I was able to save all of my tips and earnings from the gym for fun things and get caught up with debt I incurred from a relationship I had before I met Mr. Famous Bodybuilder. I felt financially free because this pampered lifestyle was amazing and I believed things couldn't get any better than they were going. He expressed his love to me and I was anticipating that he would ask me to marry him eventually.

As wonderful as things seemed to be going for us, this dream and fantasy world came to a sudden halt. It was way too good to be true. How could a man this wonderful be available? One day while he was out of town for business, this dumb ass (pardon my French, but I was mad) left his e-mail account open. Normally I don't go through a man's e-mails or phone, but his instant message box was open, and there were conversations left open as well. What woman wouldn't read it? The first message I opened read:

"Hi Big Daddy I'm missing you. My body is waiting for you to come back. It needs you; every time I touch myself I imagine it's your magical touch."

Attached to an email I opened were nude photos of a young attractive woman from Barbados who looked to be around my age as well, perhaps younger. I traveled all over the globe with him but we never went to Barbados together. He visited there often for annual doctors' conferences and I knew that he vacationed there frequently before we met because he had many souvenirs around his home and magnets on his fridge from Barbados. All day long I read through tons of emails and conversations that literally made me sick to my stomach.

One e-mail revealed to me that they were engaged! I saw that he hadn't been there in a while (probably because he was working a lot and also spending lots of time with me) but he'd send her money and gifts on a regular basis and he was expressing that he really loved her deeply and couldn't wait for them to be together again. Then I read another message, that was sent a day before he left town, that had a miscellaneous list of products that could only be obtained here in the US. She wanted these products brought to her when he arrived. There was also an explicit explanation of what she wanted to do to him sexually as soon as his plane touched down because she was missing him. She was very articulate and had a way with her words; I could definitely see why he liked her. She had a very nice body and I actually felt like I couldn't compete with her physically because she was barely five foot tall, very petite (probably just over one hundred pounds), and very gorgeous, kind of like a petite Halle Berry with a twist of Caribbean. I was a six-foot Amazon nearly double her weight and it immediately made me feel insecure about my size because maybe Dr. Grey really had a thing for more petite women (I grew up as a child hating my height and size). There was no comparison between us so I felt I couldn't compete even if I wanted to. She was petite and dainty and I was a tall and muscular athlete.

My heart dropped into my stomach, with every word I read it felt like Dr. Grey, was torturously extracting my heart from my chest with no anesthesia. I felt sharp pain and threw up several times, I was sick and depressed for days after reading all the exchanges between them; I was imagining what he was doing while he was in Costa Rica. He was out of town for "business" at a doctor's conference and this time I didn't go with him, I was staying in his home. I saw an email receipt that he purchased another plane ticket for her to meet him there during his conference. I began to cry, and then I printed out one of the girl's nude photos and stared at it. I was trying to find something physically wrong with her, some type of flaw to make me feel better but she was beautiful and as much as I didn't want to, I couldn't help but imagine what it looked like when he was making love to her. He was six foot four and she was barely over five feet with a tight body and voluptuously curvy in the right places. I was so hurt, filled with anger and released it in a very unusual way. I went into his bedroom to lie in his bed looking at her photograph, visualizing about what they were doing while he was there with her. I imagined myself being her, making love to him as I began to touch myself. I became flustered with hate and envy, thinking to myself, *this is the sensation she's feeling right now with him, she turns him on more than I do. I can't compete with her, she's tiny, has a perfect body with nice tits, and she's exotic. He's about to leave me to marry her because I'm not perfect enough for him.* Moments later, I climaxed from the strong emotions I felt of anger, jealousy, and sexual frustration toward the hurtful visions I created in my mind of him screwing her; I couldn't stop crying and beat his pillows with my fists cursing him. Feeling jealous of another woman that you believe you can't compete with was a horrible feeling and I gave into my jealousy feeling defeated. As the tears were flowing, I yelled while I thrashed my fists into the pillows, "You *asshole*! I *hate* you! You're a *liar* and a *cheater*! I hope your plane crashes on your trip back! She's younger than me and only wants you for your money you old *idiot*! You *bastard*! You're *fucking* forty-one years old and she's barely twenty! I trusted you! I *trusted* you!

Why are you doing this to me! She can never love you as much as I do or be loyal!"

After I exhausted myself from the pillow punching bags, I fell into his bed breathing hard and began to think, *I lost Dr. Grey, I am not enough for him. It's over.* There was no way I could forgive him, I felt so alone and betrayed. The feeling of death had come over me and I had to have lost over ten pounds in a matter of a few days from worrying, stressing, and not eating. I didn't know what to say or do, and I didn't call him to tell him that I knew he was cheating. I just planned to be packed up, moved out, and gone from his home before he got back from Costa Rica. I wanted to tear his house apart and burn it to the ground Left Eye style! But I didn't have the nerve to do it nor did I want to catch a criminal charge. All I could do was peacefully gather all my belongings and leave the keys to everything on the kitchen counter the day before he got back. I didn't say anything at all, no note, call, or text—nothing. I did however disarrange his house because he was Type A and hated things to be out of place. If I moved the salt shaker on his kitchen table one inch to the right he'd notice and move it back to where he wanted it; this minor thing would irritate him. He was a control freak and I knew he'd be pissed off coming in to a re-arranged and disordered house.

I ripped up the naked photograph of his Bajan Vixen, left it in his bed and left it unmade with his pillows thrown everywhere. I then began to empty out the dressers, throwing his clothes to the floor. As I emptied the clothes out of his drawers, I was shocked to find more photographs of him and another woman in a bikini on vacation together. I then found glam shots of the same girl in a professional cheerleader uniform and naked photos; she was a pro cheerleader from Atlanta! He was playing me with more than with one woman! It was sort of a relief knowing that all his energy wasn't just going into one woman he was engaged to; he was playing all of us. I ripped up the cheerleader's photos and threw the torn pieces onto his bed as well. I then re-arranged his closet by moving his shoes and clothes out of the order he had them in; threw the towels down in his master bath then wrote the word 'CHEATER' on his mirror with my lip gloss; left a pile of dirty dishes in the sink and poured a few of his favorite and expensive aged wines down the drain; I hid his salt and pepper shaker in the microwave; left his e-mails open and changed the background screensaver on his desktop computer to be one of the nude pics of his Bajan lover. It looked as if a tornado had run through his home and wish I could've been there to see his reaction because he probably had an anxiety attack; he'd unquestionably know the reason why I'd left. He was a cheater and got caught red-handed.

I didn't answer his texts or calls for weeks until he started to physically look for me. He rang my phone off the hook and would show up at my bar and my aerobics classes and at my parents' home. My mind was already made up, and all trust had gone out the window. He was fucking other women whenever he left town without me and there was nothing he could do or say to make the pain go away because I knew what the truth was already. It should have raised a red flag for me when he left his phone number with his waitress while I wasn't at work; he was a stone cold international Playboy doctor.

At this point I was through with men and through looking for love, because I felt that all men cheated and none were worth my time or energy anymore. I was on a mission to be a world player and date lots of different men from different places, and I even thought of dating women to have a better emotional bond at one point because men were such a disenchantment. They all thought with the head between their legs instead of feeling with their hearts. I wasn't going to end up hurt ever again. I was going to protect myself and my heart.

I had to leave the restaurant business because I was ready for a change and wanted to avoid Edward as much as I could, he wouldn't stop trying to come back into my life. This type of restaurant seemed to be attracting the wrong type of men to me and it reminded me of my exes. However, I felt so alive and free while I was with Dr. Grey and loved exploring different cultures around the world. I decided to become a flight attendant because when we traveled, I admired how pretty and professional they looked in uniform, especially the Emirates flight attendants, plus I loved to serve people and it would be fun to make them feel secure and comfortable. It'd be an easy transition to make from the gym and restaurant to the sky. This was such the perfect job for me (Virgos love to serve and please people) being single with no kids, having great customer service skills, a natural team leader, and a fitness instructor already knowing CPR and other lifesaving skills.

This career could easily take me away from all the pain and heartache I had been encountering with men. I was ready to travel the world on my own and meet new people and friends. I could literally live my life as a rolling stone having a man in different cities around the world and just play the unfaithful game along with them. Dating Edward got me accustomed to traveling the globe and I didn't want to stop exploring.

I had twin cousins who were flight attendants for United Airlines way before I was born and they lived in the Redondo Beach area in California. My mother told me to reach out to them and I did. They were both retired but one was still an active trainer at the airline's training academy. I told her I wanted to pursue being a flight attendant and she pointed me in the right direction and even opened her home to me if I got hired and got based in California. I also reached out to my best friend, Jessica, who used to work at the restaurant with me. She became a flight attendant for Continental Airlines, the year before, and I was so jealous of her independent lifestyle and freedom to travel the world. She could just hop on a plane and travel to exotic places whenever she had down time and I actually got to use her buddy pass a few times to travel to my fitness shows. She was the youngest flight attendant for the airline and had some amazing stories and a steady paycheck with awesome benefits and travel perks for friends and family members. The airline helped her to get her international business degree with online classes and she took her mom and brother to Rome for two weeks; I wanted to do the same thing, get paid to travel while furthering my education and still do my fitness shows. She informed that her airline wasn't currently accepting applications but gave me a website that had a list of all the other airlines that were hiring at that time. I put together my resume with a cute picture of myself on the cover letter as an attempt to stand out from other applicants and sent out over a dozen applications to the airlines I was interested in.

After a few weeks went by, I got several emails back telling me where to go for open interviews at hotels in different cities, three airlines called back, I got an invitation to a Dubai-based open interview that could totally move me to another country, and I did a couple over the phone interviews; It was narrowed down to wanting to work for Emirates, Delta, or United Airlines. I think I bombed on the first phone interview with Delta due to nervousness and then totally nailed the others. I made it to phase two of the interview process with United and had the date set up for them to fly me in for my face-to-face at the airline's headquarters in Chicago. The interview was a couple of weeks away, so my everyday hustle of fast money bartending and teaching aerobics continued. One night on the way home from the gym, something very tragic and unexpected happened that changed my plans and my life's path completely.

Feeling sleepy. This is all I can write tonight.
Signing off,
Traci

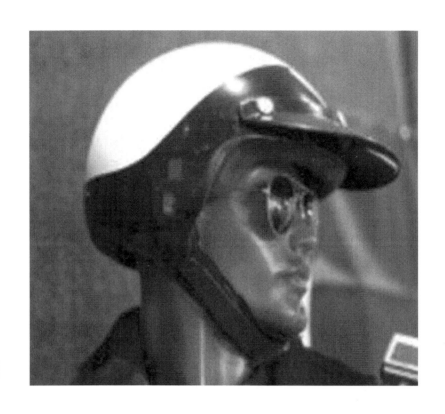

MR. STATE TROOPER

Dear Diary,

As I was driving home from the gym, I was lost in Beyonce's lyrics as I pumped her song, Me Myself and I, loud on repeat. *Me, Myself, and I, that's all I got in the end, that's what I found out, and there ain't no need to cry, I took a vow that from now on, I'm gon' be my own best friend.* There's always that perfect track for every moment in your life, this became my theme song. I began thinking about where my future as a flight attendant would take me. I was very anxious to get out of South Carolina on my own, thinking about all the new people I would meet and the places I would get to explore all while doing what I loved best, serving people. I would be helping passengers to feel comfortable and safe all while leaving my miserable love life behind in the dust and play the field for a while. I was thinking about what online university to enroll in to finish my degree while working and traveling. I was excited for my interview and anxious to learn all the new information needed to pass my FAA certification. I was up for the challenge of the face to face meeting with the airlines and my seven week training at the academy. I had already begun to teach myself basic information that all flight attendants know like all the different airport codes and teaching myself how to tell military time; I was so ready for the change.

As I turned down off the interstate onto a dark road, still singing to music and in a daydream about my new career choice to become an international Playgirl, never to find love again, I was suddenly startled by a heavy and loud impact to my truck.

"Boom!"

I hit something or rather something hit me because all I could see was open road. I looked out my driver's side rear window and I noticed it was a deer with large antlers that rammed into the side of my truck. Another car sped by and swerved on the opposite side almost striking it again. I pulled over and saw the deer faltering in the road. I'm a lover of nature and animals, and I will cry if I even hit a squirrel. I have taken an injured bird off the side of the road and brought it to an animal hospital to be cared for. I pick up turtles that walk slowly across the street and bring them to safety so they don't get run over by cars. My love for animals is deep, so imagine my reaction at hitting a large/complex animal like a deer! Animal suffering saddens me, but hitting this deer tore me to pieces! I jumped out of my SUV to see if the buck was OK; he was trying to keep himself up on his legs to make it out of the road and there was a lot of blood. I was in the street crying and trying to wave down other cars to slow down to avoid hitting him again. I was hysterical and could've gotten hit by a car myself. Luckily a sheriff deputy who lived in the same neighborhood as me was on his way home, he stopped. He put on his police lights and then grabbed me out of the road to protect me.

Out of nowhere another man appeared carrying a rifle and took aim at the buck.

I yelled, "*Please!* No! *No!* Don't shoot him!"

Bang! The sound of the gun was so loud. I fell to the ground in tears as the deer fought for his life and kicked his legs. He finally took one last breath and stopped kicking as his innocent life slipped from his shaking body; I was devastated. The man who pulled the trigger owned the house that we were in front of. He put him out of his misery with a gunshot to his head.

"The deputy said, "Good shot, sir!"

With a very heavy Southern drawl, the gunman said, "Fresh game, do ya'll wone' it? If not I'll put er' in the back of ma' truck."

The deputy said," No thanks, this young lady is pretty upset about it."

"Ma'am, it wuz the ethical thing to do cuz it wuz gon' die."

"The deputy said," Ok young lady, you have to get back in your vehicle, it's not safe for you to be out here."

I was still crying, "He *killed* him!"

"Yes. And I would have done the same. He was already bleeding to death from the impact."

"But it's my fault! I should've been driving slower to see him!"

"Deer wrecks happen all the time and you're pretty lucky, I've seen much worse, you're ok and your car appears to be drivable. It's pretty beat up on the side and you're head light is busted out so you're gonna have to get it fixed ASAP. Call the highway patrol when you get home, they'll do an accident report. You have to really drive careful and slow it down on these here dark roads. Go ahead and get in and follow behind me since we are headed the same way."

Sniffling, and trying to catch my breath I said," Yes sir."

I couldn't believe this beautiful creature had to die because of me. I just couldn't stop crying, and the deputy calmed me down enough to get back in my car and drive home. He recognized my truck and escorted me to my house since we lived in the same area. I called my parents on the way to let them know I was in a wreck and that the truck was all beat up but still drivable enough for me to bring it home.

I made it home safely, and my parents came out to assess the damage; it was pretty bad. I fell into my mother's arms as she grabbed me.

"My dad asked, "How big was this dear?"

"It was pretty big, he had huge antlers and it was really scary. I was startled, he literally charged into the truck. A man shot and killed it!"

As my mom grabbed me and kissed me, she was thanking God that I was ok. We called the highway patrol (*HP) to get an accident report for the insurance company. The dispatcher took my name, number, and address and I was told that a trooper would be coming out to do the accident report. Moments went by, and I got a call from a trooper who told me that since my vehicle was drivable, there was no need for him to come and to just go online and print out a white form and that would be all I needed for insurance purposes.

I could feel the dried up sweat on my skin and felt nasty from teaching my aerobics class so I took a long hot shower then went to my room to lie down. I began to hug my pillow still in shock and shaken up by the accident. I couldn't get the image of the man shooting the deer in its head out of my mind and seeing all that blood. I was haunted by it and kept crying because his innocent life was taken because of me. I said a prayer for the deer to rest in peace and apologized for his death. As I was finally falling asleep, I was disconcerted by my Facebook notification going off because it sounded pretty loud as I was drifting off. It was a surprising message from a friend I didn't really know. I had met this friend briefly before, maybe a couple months back, at a truck stop while I was fueling up on my way to work. His name was Curt Thomas.

His message read, "Are you OK? You had a deer wreck tonight, right?"

I was very confused because nobody knew what happened except my parents, the deputy who helped me, the country gunman, and the trooper who called me over the phone.

I replied, "Yes, I'm OK, but how did you know that I hit a deer?"

"I heard your name kalled over my radio but I was too far out to respond to the kall. I remembered having your name in my friend's list. We met at the truck stop a while ago. Do you remember?

"Yes I remember, I was running late for work that day and was very short with you. How are you?"

"I'm kool, just workin. I figured you were probably thrown off by me approaching you that day. The trooper I was with that day told me that you probably thought I was one of those kreepy Facebook stalkers, LOL. Do you need a white form? I kan bring one if you need me to bekause i'm headed back that way near where you had your wreck. We're about to do a road block in a few."

"LOL no, I didn't think you were creepy, I'm sorry if I came off abrupt or rude. I was running late and couldn't talk to you that day. I think I remember you having some cute dimples. The trooper who called me on the phone tonight told me to go to your website and download the white form so you don't need to trouble yourself. I can print it out here at home, thanks for offering to help though."

At that moment I decided to go through his Facebook page and look at his posts and all his pictures. He was very handsome and seemed like a pretty cool guy. His relationship status said single and I saw no signs of him being involved in a relationship by going through all his photos. I remember falling asleep that night and then waking up to another Facebook message from him.

"Hey, I noticed you're a biology major and you go to Klaflin, that's wassup. I'm almost finished with nursing skool…glad to see you have brains and not just a pretty face with a body…in kase you're wondering, yea I'm a State Trooper but I'm also gonna to be a nurse, I'm a medic in the Air Force too! I am a man of many uniforms LOL."

He wrote all his "C" sounding words with a "K" and I found it to be pretty strange.

"Wow! That's impressive. You do it all! You're a trooper, a nurse, and an Airman? You must be a Virgo, because only a Virgo would have that many service titles. Also, why do you write all your C's as K's?"

"How'd you guess? Oh... Duh, my birthday is in my profile. Using a "K" in place of a "C" is a Kappa thing my Frat does. When is your birthday?"

"No, actually I really did just guess. You come off as a Virgo man and I'm a Virgo in September too, I think I like you already! So you're a Greek huh? I was thinking about joining back when I went to school in Maryland but the sorority I wanted to join was so mean and stuck up there. They used to make the girls have fundraisers to buy them designer things like purses and shoes. It was funny and all but I didn't want to go through all that just to be part of them. I was a bit intimidated and just decided to stay "Me Phi Me" while I was there! LOL"

"LOL I hear ya. What sorority was it?"

"AKA."

"Oh, they're not so bad, it's a process you have to go through to be initiated and then it's real kool after that. You may want to just wait and join the grad chapter. Historically, AKA's have done a lot for the kommunity and the world."

"Really? Well maybe I'll look into it more because I don't know any of the sorority girls here and they may be nicer. I don't really have many female friends. Sigma Gamma Rho and Delta Sigma Theta are pretty big up North where I'm from. I may look into them as well."

"Oh word? Where up North are you from? Sigma Gamma Rho is my sister sorority. If you join I think you would be a good one. Just do your research on them first and choose the one that interests you the most and don't choose for kolors!"

"Ok LOL! I will read up on them. I'm from New York btw."

"The city?"

"LOL, why does everyone here always ask that? No, I'm not from New York City. I'm from White Plains which is about 45 minutes from the city, it's in Westchester County."

We began conversing pretty often and found out that we had so much in common. We finally exchanged cell phone numbers and took it from Facebook to the phone. We connected on a very deep level. We sent nearly one hundred thousand text messages (not kidding either) over the course of two weeks and it was a never ending thing. I was very excited, and he was a breath of fresh air for me. We were so in tune with one another, it was almost telepathic, we would finish each other's sentences and knew what was on each other's minds. We both spoke about heartbreaks and infidelity that we had experienced. Our conversations quickly began to get really heated and sexually explicit in nature.

"Where you at babygirl? Been thinking about you all day. Still at work? I'm jealous of all those guys who get to be in your presence right now."

"Hey love! I'm just getting off. I'm jealous of all the women who are lucky enough to be stopped by you and be in your presence. Matter of fact I'm going to make it back to Orangeburg in twenty five minutes! Come get me because I'm about to break the law! I want you to pull me over for speeding!"(It really took 40- 50 minutes for me to get home)

"Not on my interstate you won't! I'll pull you over real quick and lock your pretty ass up for reckless driving. I don't play that, ask any of my co-workers about me. I don't care how fine you are, you break the law, you're going to jail."

"Mmm! Damn, I love how stern you are. I'd like that and I want you to cuff me and be very rough with me! I'm being a bad girl speeding down the highway screamin' Fuck the Law! LOL."

"Yeah, you're about to get *fucked* by the law alright but seriously don't speed babygirl. I'll swing by to see you're fine ass when you get here. Hit me up when you're home and I'll kome over for a few."

"Ok. I have to shower first because I smell like hot wings and french fries! LOL."

Visits to my home became a regular occurrence while he was on duty in his patrol car. We would be parked for hours in his car on my parents' driveway at three and four o'clock in the morning after I'd get home from working night shift at the restaurant. I'd either wear my work uniform with sweats or very revealing and transparent clothing leaving little to his imagination. I wanted to turn him on. Eye contact was such a turn on for me, and I'd stare deep into his eyes and feel passion heating up in both of us. I loved being able to see the lust he had for me and could always tell he wanted me bad. Our relationship grew from innocent conversations to actual heated seduction really fast! It was electrical; I'd try to talk to him like I was his sexy dispatcher telling him where to go and what I wanted him to do to me. I looked up his trooper 10-codes on the internet (radio codes that law enforcement and firefighters use to communicate over the radio) to flirt with him.

"Ok baby, I'm home and fresh out the shower, what's your 10-20 (location) and 10-26 (estimated arrival time)? I want you to come 10-69 (detain) me for being a bad girl today."

"I'm 10-17 right now babygirl and I'm gonna 10-69 that ass for sure when I get there!"

"Copy that, 10-4."

We turned each other on so much, our first kiss felt so powerful and passionate, I remember moaning at the first taste of his lips. His hands moved up my arms and to my shoulders, pulling down my tank top and exposing my breasts. The cool breeze from the lowered driver side window moved over my skin, giving me goose bumps all over and making my nipples hard. He grabbed my breasts, squeezed them together, and then began to lick his warm tongue across my sensitive nipples. He discovered my spot, it felt so good I moaned and I gripped his head tighter as he ran his tongue slowly around my areolas to tease me. I arched my back in pleasure, pushing more of my breast into his mouth. He saw how turned on I was; he reached his hand into my Victoria's Secret sweat pants, felt how wet I was, and used my wetness to caress soft and gentle circles on my clit. I was so turned on by his touch, he was so mild and very passionate with me; I wanted to jump his bones so bad! He was on the clock and this was really happening in his patrol car! He was so sexy and made me feel super-hot, encounters with him were like the soft-core scenes you'd see on the Playboy or Spice channel.

As I began to climax we heard his code name called over his radio, "Z-007, 10-20?"(Using Z-007 to protect the area's code names)

In a deep voice, Curt said, "Z-007."

The woman dispatcher said," Go ahead, Z-007."

There was a bunch of police jargon being exchanged between him and dispatch after he gave his location, then he abruptly told me that he had to leave right away. I pulled up my tank top and kissed him on the cheek telling him to be careful. He cut his blue lights on and sped out of the driveway into darkness. My heart was beating fast as I watched until I could no longer see his lights flashing in the distance worried for his safety, but he's been a trooper for a while so I'm sure he was used to responding to calls. If he got called to work a wreck or to do a roadblock or high speed chase, he would always come back to me when he was finished if he didn't have to take somebody to jail. He left me in a daze; I couldn't believe he was able to make me climax without having sex with me. A man this fine and gifted at pleasing me was just too good to be true! His touch was so amazing and I wanted to feel him inside me so bad. The suspense of waiting to have sex was really building up the sexual tension between us. Thoughts and fantasies of him raced my mind daily, he gave me life and the bond between us was incredible.

I laid in bed worried, waiting for him to call me or text that he was OK and coming back. His job made me so uneasy because you never knew what can happen on each shift; the interstate is a crazy place to work. As I was falling asleep I got a text asking if I was still awake. I was sleepy but I told him to come back anyway. When he pulled up, I got back into his patrol car and gave him a big hug and kiss telling him I always get nervous when he rushes to calls. Then I said, "Baby, you changed my plans. If we didn't meet I'd be in Chicago right now and then off to the flight attendant academy for seven weeks. You're something special and I can feel it. I don't want to go away anymore; I'm going to stay here with you. I'm afraid to tell you this and don't want to scare you but I think I'm falling for you! I lust you!"

"You better not go anywhere! I feel the same way baby, something is different. There's no pretending. I lust you too."

"Yeah, it just feels unforced and natural. We are flowing; I really think you're the one baby!"

"Same here."

We said "lust" even though we both wanted to say love, but it was so sudden, it was very scary to have such a strong feeling so soon. We had such a strong connection mentally, physically, and spiritually. It just felt so meant to be, like we were written in the stars to be together. The tragic death of that innocent deer gave birth to our union together. It was like a sacrifice from the Universe to unite our hearts. If that wreck never happened, I don't know how we would have met because I had grown to be cynical about love and really about to become a world class flight attendant Playgirl. Needless to say, I never made it to my interview with United Airlines because I fell deeply in love with this man.

I relocated to a health club that just opened up closer to my home so I could avoid Dr. Grey who would show up to take my classes at my old gym. This new fitness center allowed me to teach a lot more classes and I helped to structure the group fitness and set the standard for other instructors who got hired. Our programs were very challenging and the members loved it! I got more certifications to teach new classes and the group fitness was booming. I switched to working mostly morning shifts at the restaurant so I could have energy to spend time with my new found love.

It awkwardly seemed that he only came to see me while he was working night shift and I told him that I wanted to be with him off the clock. It didn't happen right away but after having several nightly rendezvous with my dream guy, we planned a night out on the town with him being out of his uniform. It was a Friday, and we finally went on our first official date to a restaurant called Bonefish Grill, which became our favorite place to dine out. We were so natural that anyone looking in on us would've assumed we'd been together for years. We had fallen for each other very quickly—so quickly that he failed to mention some things about himself that would have automatically been a deal breaker for me.

I'm so intrigued by this man.
Love,
Traci

CHAPTER 4

PATIENCE

Dear Diary,

On our first date, Curt seemed to be struggling picking up his food with his chopsticks trying to use both of his hands instead of one, so I gave him a quick lesson on how to properly use them. Once he got the hang of it he began to feed me *bang bang* shrimp and I also fed him from my sticks as well. We weren't going to drink but I talked him into trying a pomegranate martini with me. Once the waiter brought our drinks, I proposed a toast to our new found love.

"It feels like we hit the lottery. Cheers to us for finding love in a world where people play games, lying and cheating and sleeping around with so many different people and we are protected from all of that now. We have each other. The game is over and we won! Cheers to our future!"

We tapped our glasses together and took a sip. He suddenly grabbed my hand and gave me a very serious look. I gave him the same serious stare back and then smiled asking him what was wrong?

He asked, "How patient are you?" I looked confused because I didn't understand his question or why he was asking that.

"Patient about what, Curt?"

He then changed the subject, but his question stayed heavily on my mind.

"Do you want dessert babygirl?"

"Sure, let's split the calories of a brownie and ice cream or chocolate cake. We can work it off later!"

"OK cool."

Everything continued perfectly that evening, and we were so head over heels. We had gotten so many compliments from people about how great we looked together as a couple. He was so sexy to me! Everything about him turned me on so much, even his car turned me on because it fit his personality so well. He had the hottest looking silver Mustang, which was personalized with his Greek fraternity, Kappa Alpha Psi, engraved in raised silver lettering on the sides near the front wheels. The interior was black leather, and I had never been inside a Mustang before. It was a stick shift and I began to flirt with him when we got back in his car.

"Can you teach me how to drive your stick? I've been dying to learn and wanted to take it for a test drive to see if I can handle it."(I meant that in the most sexual seductive way possible) He told me to place my left hand on top of his hand to help guide his shifting.

As he guided my hand he said," Close your eyes and listen to the sound of the engine. When you hear it and then feel the vibration lighten up, apply pressure to the clutch and then gently slide the stick down to the next gear then release the clutch. It's almost sexual; you need to be in tuned with your body and the car."

The way he was explaining how to drive it was making me really hot, I moved my hand from his stick to between his legs as he began to accelerate. He revved the loud engine up and switched through gears showing me how fast it could go while we were on the open road. In my mind I was thinking *don't you pull people over and give tickets for doing this?* I assume he wasn't worried about being stopped because the highway literally was his office. I guess every job has its perks! It was really turning me on.

He pulled us over to the shoulder of the interstate, and we started kissing and fondling as other cars zoomed by us going seventy miles an hour and faster. It was such a rush. I was worried that a highway patrol-man from another county would stop us because we were outside of the area that he patrolled, but if he wasn't worried, then I guessed it was OK. The suspense of thinking we could get caught and the power he had being a trooper turned me on so much. I reached between his legs again and felt how hard he was. I could tell he wanted to make me come again, but it was my turn to return the favor. As he was reaching to undo my shirt, I grabbed his hand and whispered in his ear, "I want to taste you."

I began to kiss his neck as I unzipped his jeans and pulled out his erection. I'd felt it before through his uniform, but this was my first time actually seeing it. It was perfectly circumcised and quite larger than I had anticipated. I began to pleasure him. Moments later he let out a grunt/moan as he grabbed my hair tightly and climaxed into my mouth; he was shaking.

As I was wiping my mouth, I said to him, "Mmm. I can tell you eat healthy; your come tastes so sweet!" He looked at me like he couldn't believe what I just did and said.

"I do eat a lot of fruit but *damn* girl! How'd you learn to give such a great blowjob?"

I laughed and said, "OH, I never told you huh? Well that's yet another thing I'm certified to do besides fitness!"

"Say what?"

"Ha ha! I'm just kidding babe. You'd be surprised what you can find on the net. I actually did a lot of research about giving good head and how to find all the sensitive spots. I really wanted to return the favor and make you feel as good as you make me feel all the time."

"Damn girl! You are definitely a keeper. Can you cook too? You know I'm a country boy right? Cuz we love to eat!"

"Ha ha! I can throw down a little bit. I bake a mean lasagna! I'll make you one for our next date instead of us going out to eat."

"Ok cool. I can't go out like this, I'm going to have to return the favor and eat you for my dessert!"

"Ha ha! Sounds good to me! I'll bring the whipped cream."

He drove me back home, and I really wanted to spend the night with him, but he seemed to be taking his dear sweet time with me. His procrastination to have sex with me was such a turn on and I just wanted to pounce on him even more!

Curt was so devilishly handsome, and he wore his trooper uniform the best I have ever seen. State Troopers in South Carolina have one of the sharpest looking uniforms in this country, the colors look really really good but Curt made them look even better. Most troopers here and in other states I have seen, wear them loosely fitted or just let them fit however they'd fit naturally to their body without any alterations; Curt on the other hand was true to his Virgo sign and was a perfectionist to the core. It could have been the discipline from his Air Force training but he looked absolutely flawless, like a male model. He got his uniforms tailored to fit him like a glove, and you could see how fit his body was underneath. His ass looked so good in his uniform that I actually witnessed women swerve in the road nearly crashing their cars trying to get a good look at him as he worked traffic stops and wrecks (yes I used to spy on him while he worked, I was infatuated!). Curt seriously looked like a fantasy male escort or adult entertainer in his uniform. The type of man a woman would visualize pulling her over for naughty pleasures; he had the body, complexion, haircut, smile, and dimples resembling the sexy R&B singer, Usher Raymond. Physically, Curt was the best-looking man I'd ever dated and I was besotted by his charm. He had the nerve to have the nickname *Kryptonite* because he certainly was my weakness, he got the name from his Greek fraternity, notorious for having "Sexy Pretty Boys" or as they call themselves, "Nupes."

He got hit on daily from "fast" women, literally and figuratively; he told me stories of how he'd see women trying to fix themselves up with makeup as he approached their cars on traffic stops. He said sometimes professional women would try to slip him their business cards and have their skirts hiked way up; lots of cleavage showing and he could smell fresh perfume that was sprayed before getting to their window. There was always a microphone or camera rolling so he always remained professional with the heavy advances from them. He had a reputation for being very mean and stern, not caring how good a woman looked. If she was in the wrong, she'd get a ticket or go to jail depending on the violation. He even gave a ticket to a famous video vixen who is very well known in the music industry and had appeared in many hip hop videos. She was speeding in an exotic car on her way to make an appearance at a nightclub and he stopped her. She went as far as getting out her car claiming her license was in a bag in her trunk, just so she could get out her car to show off her voluptuous body. She was dressed very provocative and he knew who she was but didn't care, she wasn't getting out of the summons because she was a "hot chick". He was very callous towards women trying to get by on their looks. He was a keeper; not once did I feel the need to feel insecure or worry about another woman stealing him away from me. I have never felt so much joy and passion being in the company of a man like I did while I was with him. I knew he was the one I would marry; I could feel so much passion in our kisses.

On our next date, I baked lasagna for him with a side salad and set up a candle light dinner outdoors. It was so beautiful and romantic and under the stars. I had soft r&b playing with some red wine and he really enjoyed my cooking. I guess the saying is true that the way to a man's heart is through his stomach because it felt like he was ready to take our relationship to the next level. We had been dating for a few weeks before we decided to become totally intimate and completely sexually active. On this night, we set a date to spend an entire weekend together in a nice hotel suite. We were so excited and anxious for the day to arrive for us to go. A couple days before we had our romantic weekend, he dropped a huge bomb on me, a bomb that would have made any other woman in her right mind close up shop and walk away.

"I have something to tell you Traci and I'm not sure how you are going to take it."

"What Curt? You can tell me anything, I love you."

"Promise you won't flip and get mad?"

I was getting nervous because he was really serious and seemed to have something very important to tell me. I said, "I promise baby, just say it. What's on your mind?"

"Well, I'm legally married and I live in the same house as my wife."

"*What*! You're joking right? Nah, you're playing with me."

"I'm not, I'm legally married."

"Ha ha! This is funny! OK so... where are the Punked cameras because this better be a joke. You're joking right? This is really a prank?"

"It's the truth Traci, and I'm sorry, I was trying to find the right time to tell you without scaring you away and I didn't expect to fall in love. My wife and I aren't really together. We live in the same house and have marriage papers, but it's been a dead relationship for so long."

I was thinking to myself, *"OH my God! I was messing around and fell in love with a married man! Why did he pursue me? Why play with my heart and lead me on to think we could have a future together?* I was ready to crawl back into my protective shell and pull my disappearing act on him. I felt beyond betrayed and I had already canceled my interview with the airlines that was meant to help me escape from the heartache and pain of love and hurt from bad relationships.

Curt confided in me that the marriage was very cold and said that they currently slept in different rooms. He also said that he loved her for being the mother to his son but that they have grown apart over the years and he has been living as if he was single and had been seeing other women. He had the title of being a "husband" but hasn't been living up to it and staying together as husband and wife to keep a stable family environment for their son. He also told me he stayed in the marriage because his parents were pastors and he didn't want to hurt his mother by leaving his family.

"So wait a minute, you have a child together too?"

"Yes, that's the main reason why we are still together. We actually don't see each other much, only in passing."

He told me she was a school teacher and worked days, while he worked a lot of nights. He was very convincing, and I was already so in love with him. I could feel his love was real for me too and that he wasn't playing me like he had done to the women before me. I let everything about the situation soak in for a little bit and then went ahead and received it for what it was. I tried to be understanding of what he was going through, I mean, I thought I was a pretty good catch and the other men in my life didn't realize it until I was gone! Curt saw my worth right away and had no choice but to fall for me too! He was in a situation that he wanted out of, and when we met everything just seemed so right between us. There was just something about him that I couldn't let go of and walk away. We both felt like we were in our own world together, and our connection was totally unexpected.

Curt's initial intention was to have a fling and then move on. He was a player, and he was honest about letting me know that he messed with other women during his marriage. He was so honest that he shared a Faccbook mcssage he had exchanged with another law enforcement officer from another city. The message said that he made me give him a blow job and that he was going to hit it soon and then dump me to the curb and they were laughing and joking about it. I got upset when he showed me this conversation they had about me; he just wanted prove to me that no other woman has had him whipped like me and that playing me like a game were his intentions.

Curt was the very definition of a Playboy and liked to date different women knowing none of the relationships would go anywhere past being physical; connecting with me was a game changer because I wasn't just a fling to him, I was a keeper. He retired his player card; meeting me put an end to his days as a cold Casanova and he stopped me dead in my tracks from becoming a sexual libertine like he was.

Moving forward, I allowed him to book our weekend getaway, and we planned an awesome weekend of dining in bed, crazy love making for three days and really exploring one another. Our connection was so real; he totally understood my body and exactly how to touch me, talk to me, and connect with me. His fraternity was notorious for being good at pleasing women, and he sure did live up to those expectations. We were both givers, and it was almost a battle trying to please one another. We were both fighting to be in control; it was like a sexual marathon, there were no seats or armrests in the way or restraints from being in uniform; no parts of my body were off limits to him. We both came quite quickly and then began to relax and connected on an even deeper level.

After our first round of intense love making was over, I straddled his lap and he entered into my body again. After all the sexual tension we had built up was released, we began to move slowly and naturally channeled our sexual energy. Soft music was playing in the background; I'd inhale while he exhaled. I'd consciously take his breath into my body as I stared deep into his eyes with each slow and deep stroke inside me; he did the same and we began to breathe as one as our energy flowed through each other. His arms were wrapped around my waist while mine were around his neck; our eyes were locked and I could literally see the stars in the Universe by gazing into his eyes. He was so dreamy and took me away from reality. Our intimacy was like a journey through inter-stellar space and we were giving each other the energy from our hearts and soul. We both gave each other orgasm after orgasm and lost count.

This was the best intimacy I have ever had that went way beyond just physical pleasure. After we connected sexually, it was official. We were soul mates destined to find one another, and we could feel it in our touch because it was bigger than life; it was bigger than the both of us. Our lovemaking was deeper than just physical pleasure because we just naturally landed into Kama Sutra positions and breathing techniques that couples usually have to read about and study to perform efficiently. Most people just screw each other and only connect physically but we had a natural spiritual bond; it felt as if our souls were finally reunited after being apart for some time. It was Tantric and time stood still for us, we were in bliss.

On the second day of our romantic weekend, he went down to the restaurant to get us breakfast. While he was gone, the phone rang in our room. I thought it was him calling to ask me a question about the food selection, so I answered it. To my surprise a woman was on the other end. She asked, "May I speak to Curt?"

"He's not here. He went to get breakfast."

"Is this Traci?"

I thought to myself, *Oh boy, what is this?* I said, "Yes, this is Traci. Who is this?"

"This is Curt's wife. Tell him that his son is waiting for him to come home and that I hope he won't be disappointing him again." She then hung up the phone on me, and I was in shock. I knew about her already, but I was in shock because, if everything Curt told me was the truth, then why would she be calling us at the hotel? How did she know we were there and why would she care?

When Curt got back to our room with breakfast, I told him that his wife called, and our weekend ended immediately. We didn't even get to touch our breakfast.

"Get dressed and pack your things. We have to get back ASAP."

"Why what's wrong? What's going on Curt?"

"This is the 'patient' part I was asking you about before, just bear with me and trust me baby."

I got dressed and packed my things knowing something was wrong with the situation. There was nothing but silence as we drove back into town. His whole demeanor changed after his wife called and I felt foolish, betrayed and heartbroken for trusting him and his words. Why would he be rushing to get home? Something just wasn't right and I needed answers.

Feeling deceived,
Traci

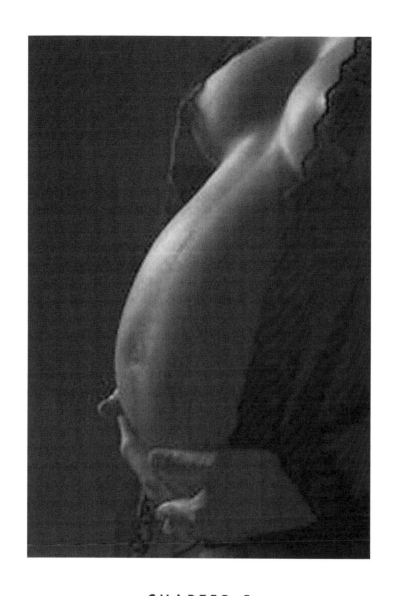

CHAPTER 5

BABY BOMBSHELL

Dear Diary,

Curt sent me a text later on that evening apologizing and told me that he would come by to see me the next day, Sunday. When he came by, he apologized again and told me he really needed me to be patient with the situation. He knew he really wanted to be serious with me and that I wasn't a fling. He told me that he didn't want to lose me and was going to look for an apartment to finally move out the house. I was happy, but I didn't believe it until I actually saw him do it. I'd been so hurt by men, and it just seemed I couldn't catch a break! All the men in my life had been liars and cheaters! I also asked him when he planned on starting the divorce process because he never seemed to bring it up. His answer was that he couldn't file for divorce right away because in South Carolina, a man can't divorce his wife while she is pregnant and that he'd need to do a paternity test to prove that the baby didn't belong to him. I nearly dropped dead after receiving this new baby bombshell. I was so filled with emotion that tears began to roll down my cheeks.

"What? She's pregnant? Why are you just now telling me this?" I had *no clue* his wife was expecting!

"She had to have gotten tired of me being unfaithful and decided to do her own thing too. The baby isn't mine, the timing just isn't adding up."

"Why are you just telling me this now? You just keep dropping these bombs on me Curt! What's next huh? Withholding truth is just as bad as lying to me! What else haven't you told me yet, Curt? I don't know what could be much worse than having a wife who is pregnant! This is horrible and I don't think my heart can take much more. You're one hundred percent sure that the baby she carries is not your child?"

He told me he was ninety-nine percent sure it wasn't, they had been intimate months ago but he speculated she was with someone else. His story was that he was away for two weeks air force training in Texas during the time that the baby was conceived, according to her due date and his calculations. I was devastated and hurt, but trusted his words, especially when he finally found himself an apartment and moved out the house. It added credibility to his story because what type of man would move out from his wife's house while she's pregnant? I actually felt sorry for their situation thinking and believing that they both wanted out of their marriage but couldn't because of the legalities of her expecting. I wanted to stick by his side and go through it with him. I mean, if they were both dating outside of marriage and she was pregnant by another man, then there was no reason why I should walk away right? I thought to myself, *This is just a legal situation, there are no feelings involved, she probably wants to be with the father of her child. They are just married on paper and now she's pregnant by her lover who isn't Curt.* I loved him dearly, and I was ready to ride out this challenging time in his life with him.

I moved into his new apartment a few weeks later, and it was really good. We were so inseparable. He would come to my gym and watch me teach my classes, wait for me to finish, and escort me to my car. He would also show up at my other job and watch me mix drinks and make sure nobody was flirting with me. He was so very protective of me, and I loved it. He was my best friend, and even more, he was my soul mate. We actually got soul mate rings with the words *Mo Anam Cara*, engraved around the bands for each other. They looked like wedding rings and we also engraved our name and birthdays on the inside. We couldn't be married on paper right away but we were definitely married in spirit after we united our body and souls sexually.

He supported all my dreams and accompanied me to my fitness competitions and would even purchase competitor entries to get a tag to be backstage with me, even though he wasn't competing in the show. He wanted to be backstage with me to make sure nobody would mess with me. We never spent one day apart from one another, totally inseparable.

As time passed many people in our town began to know about our relationship because it wasn't kept a secret. We allowed ourselves to be seen out publicly, and he was regularly seen at my job. Many knew he was a married man with a pregnant wife, but nobody said anything. For the most part, people liked seeing us together. They saw that we were happy and that everything seemed to be so perfect between us.

I did, however, begin to feel guilty and felt empathy for his wife because I felt sorry for her situation. I couldn't imagine being a pregnant woman and being alone. What type of woman could let a man as fine and perfect as Curt get away? He obviously had to love her at some point in their relationship. In my mind I was thinking that if I were in her shoes, I'd be very depressed and probably suicidal. I felt so bad for the situation that I wanted to contact her because I just couldn't wrap my brain around it. I began thinking to myself, *"Was Curt telling me the truth about everything or was there another side to the story that was missing?"* I really wanted some answers so I told Curt about my concern, but he insisted I not worry about it and not to attempt any contact with her. What gave me piece of mind about her situation was thinking that she really wasn't alone and that she had the man who fathered the child she carried. I was just anxious for both of them to be freed from the messy situation they were in.

The months went by, and the time finally came for his wife to deliver her baby. He received the call early in the morning to go to the hospital, and he had to leave me. I was so depressed because he was there with her, and of course, there was a chance that the baby was his. I was praying that it wasn't his child and praying for the time to pass quickly so that he could come back to be with me.

When he finally came back home, he didn't say a word to me. He just got back into bed and seemed like he didn't want to speak to me; I let him sleep. Later on that day, he finally told me that the baby resembled his first born but that he still needed a paternity test to be sure if he belonged to him or not. This situation was getting way too "Maury Povich" for me, I felt very on edge about it and I was scared. I began thinking *what's going to happen to us if this is his baby?*

After a few weeks went by, they did a paternity test, and Curt and I anxiously waited for the results to be mailed back so that we could hopefully begin our new life together. The day finally came and we got the package in the mail.

Holding a big white envelope in his hand, Curt said, "Here it is."

"I'm scared that these results will make us or break us as a couple. What if it's your baby?"

"If he's mine, I'm not going anywhere like you think I am. Baby we are soulmates and this won't keep us apart. Things will be a little complicated for a while but we will be together. Do you want to open it or do you want me to open it?"

I took a deep breath in and said, "No, you open it."

There was nothing but silence as Curt carefully and slowly tore open the envelope. He pulled out a stack of papers and we both looked over them. There was a lot of medical jargon that I didn't understand but he did.

"What does all this mean? Where's the part that says if he's yours?"

He said," Traci, he's mine!"

"What? I thought you were so certain Curt! You said ninety-nine percent! You lied to me! You left her and that was your child!" I felt like my soul had been ripped from my body once again, I felt nauseated.

"I'm going to see him, I have to, that's my seed, and I'm glad he's mine."

"You're going over to her house?"

"Yes, those are my boys."

He told me that he felt relieved that the baby was his son because he didn't want to confuse his oldest having to explain having a half-brother. I didn't sign up for this type of drama or pain and I just knew for sure that Curt would go back with his wife to be a family.

"Go then! I seriously hope you two rekindle your broken marriage. I'm out of here!"

I grabbed my swimsuit and goggles then threw them in my gym bag, snatched my choreography notes off the DVD player, and stormed out. I went to the gym to blow off some steam. As I was passing the front desk, the woman working told me that they just installed new sound systems and that I needed a key to access them. She told me to sign my name and then handed me a small key. I went into the spin room and hooked my iPod up to the new system. It sounded amazing! I closed the door and blasted my music loud as I began to ride and practice my choreography. After a couple hours, the director came in and told me that he was jamming to my music but that I needed to turn it down a bit. He then asked if I liked the new equipment and engaged into a conversation with me.

He said," And that's why you're our best instructor. You're the only one I see who comes in to practice for hours like this. We are going to have to name this gym after you because you nearly teach everything and take up the entire schedule! Management is changing over the next few months. I'll make sure to put in a good word about promoting you to be over group fitness to the new director who will be taking over this facility. Everyone just raves about your classes, keep it up!"

"Thanks! It's my passion to be here and I'd love to run the Group X, I hope the new guy is as cool as you. Well, I'm done now, sorry I had the music so loud, and yes, the new sound system and wireless headsets are awesome! Sounds really amazing!"

"Yea it was expensive too! Don't forget to put the mic back in the cage and lock up. Return the key to the front desk and you have a good afternoon."

"No problem, I'm done for the day. I'm about to hit the pool for a few laps. See you tomorrow!"

"Where do you get all that energy from? Whatever you're on I need some!"

"Ha ha! I work out when I'm under stress or feel anxiety. It helps to calm my nerves."

"Well whatever it is I hope you feel better. Enjoy your swim!"

"Thanks."

Little did my boss, or any of my co-workers know about the drama I was going through with my man, who I used to boast so much about. I was there busting my ass, pissed off trying to keep my mind from thinking about Curt being with his wife and kids. I drowned out my worries and frustrations with fitness and nobody knew what I was going through, I felt so alone. Curt was my best friend and I had no other outlets besides working out.

When I got to the pool, I saw one of my fellow pump instructors enjoying the jets in the hot tub. She was a Figure Competitor and also a member of Team Bombshell. When I saw her, I deviated to the whirl pool instead of swimming laps. Her eyes were closed and she had on headphones. As I walked down the steps to get in, I called her name. She didn't hear me so walked over and tapped her on the shoulder. I must've scared her because she jumped unexpectedly and startled me too nearly pulling her iPod into the water. "Oh hey! What's up Skinny Minnie? (Her nickname for me) You bout damn gave me a heart attack sneakin' up on me like that wit yo high yellow ass!"

Laughing I said, "My Bad! I didn't mean to scare you. Girl you're so funny! Did you learn the new release yet?

"The new release? Heck no. I been workin' so much and haven't had time to even look at it yet. The package is still sitting unopened in my car, I know you already know it though super star! Is the music any good?"

"It's cool. You know the songs always grow on you after listening to them over and over again. There's a couple cool tracks and some fun new moves too. We should practice with Z, later because he's thinking about getting certified on this new release. Girl, I'm so stressed."

"Uh oh. What's wrong now Skinny Minnie?"

"I'm too through with Curt. Remember when I told you he was married? Well, come to find out, that wasn't everything. There was more baggage."

"Well darn, what else was there?"

"Girl, his wife was also pregnant and we just got the results back today that it's his son! The only reason I stayed in a relationship with him is because he told me his wife was pregnant by another man. Guess it was a lie."

"Damn! That sounds like some Maury Povich shit."

"Precisely, that's exactly what I said! He's over to her house now and I just don't know how to handle all of this drama! I'm about to have a breakdown."

I needed someone to vent to and she was always really down to earth and non-judgmental so I told her all about everything. She actually gave me some good advice because she too had gone through a similar situation before.

"Traci, Blended families are the families of the future, there's a lot of it going around. If you really love him, you're going to have to get used to being a stepmom." She encouraged me to stay strong and told me that if Curt really loved me, that having another child won't change the way he feels. "Keep your head up Skinny Minnie, stay focused on what you've got going on. You're looking leaner are you cutting? When's your next show? I'm done competing for the year; I'm enjoying my off season focused on adding more bulk!"

"I'll try; it's hard to stay focused. I'm doing Nationals in Miami, twelve weeks out. I'm really stressed though and not eating enough to hold my muscle. I'm thinking about leaving South Carolina, there's really no reason to stay if things don't work out."

"Follow your heart, if it's meant to be then it will be. If not, fuck it! You're young and I'd leave too if I had no ties here! Haha!"

"Well if he's still at the house with his wife when I get back I'm going to make moves to leave. You're right. Fuck it! I'm too young for this type of drama."

After talking with her I decided to head back home to our apartment, hoping that he would be there waiting for me. It had to have been almost five hours that I was gone. I stopped by Chick-Fil-A to get grilled chicken nuggets and a large fruit cup because I didn't prep my food and was starving by the time I finished all that working out. By the time I came back home I lost my appetite. I saw his Mustang was still gone; I knew he was still visiting with his wife and kids.

Feeling down.
Signing off until next time,
Traci

CHAPTER 6

MIAMI: STAGED PREGNANCY

Dear Diary,

After this new baby bombshell, our relationship began to get cold. I couldn't take the fact that he would go over to her house to be with the baby. It wasn't really the fact that he went over there; it was the time of day that he went. He'd go early in the morning to see his oldest son get on the school bus and then go inside to see the newborn baby. In the morning, most women aren't dressed appropriately and skimpy; in my opinion, it's just as bad as going late at night. I didn't know if she was desperate to have him back or not so I pictured that she'd be wearing very little clothing when he'd come by and make sure she was looking her best. At least, that's what I would do if I was her and wanted him back. Also from what he told me, she had lost all her baby weight pretty fast and was back down to pre baby size already, so she wasn't looking bad at all.

I've seen her before she was pregnant not knowing who she was until Curt told me. She actually took one of my classes before and she was very attractive and also naturally a very small and petite woman. I began having flashbacks of Dr. Grey and his Bajan lover; that feeling of jealousy and insecurity began to consume my mind again because Curt's wife shared the same body type as the Barbadian girl; petite and curvy. The thought of Curt going back to his wife and being intimate was making me sick to my stomach; I've been cheated on in every relationship before and Curt was married so why would this situation be any different; my mind was already conditioned for him to leave me. I was done and ready to move on with my life to become a flight attendant. I looked up the airlines that were hiring and began to resubmit applications and send resumes again. I wanted to leave him before he could leave me. I was thinking, *he's going to eventually return back to be with her so they could be a family*; I was insecure and jealous of the connection (children) they had and wanted to get out of the state or better yet the country, so I wouldn't have to deal with it anymore.

As I waited to hear back from the airlines, I put all my focus on preparing for my next fitness show, thinking that our relationship would eventually fall apart. But to my surprise, he never left me, and he did let me know that he was really done with the situation and wanted to move forward with me and our life.

On my way to work at the restaurant one evening, he stopped me before I got into my car and said, "Traci, I don't want you working there anymore. I want to take care of you. Just focus on your fitness shows and teaching at the gym. Don't go in to work today; let's go out to eat in Charleston tonight."

"But I need the money Curt and how do I know you're not going to go back to your wife? I'm just getting really tired of the situation and I need to work, me quitting isn't going to make anything better for me. I'm actually thinking of getting another job now."

"I know, I saw your emails to the airlines. You obviously left them open on the computer for me to see. So you've already planned to leave me to be a flight attendant?"

"Yes, I can't deal with this anymore, I know you have kids together but I don't like sharing you with her. I don't know what you do when you go over there and I'd like it to stop. If you love me, you'll find another way to see your boys because that's so disrespectful to me and our relationship. You're in her house! How does that look you going in there and it's just you two with a newborn? She's breastfeeding right? Why don't you picture this. How would you feel if I had kids by my ex, Dr.Grey, and he came over to my house early in the morning with just me and our new born and I was breastfeeding and dressed in pajamas? Oh and I had my body back looking tight with a new mom glow. That'd be cool right? I would tell you that he's just coming over to see his newborn. Oh and we don't talk, he just holds his son, would you believe me and feel comfortable with it even if it was the truth? That's just way too much Curt, either you find another way or I'm gone. I'm not going to stay here and watch this, there's nothing in this town for me besides you and there's a big world of opportunity out there for me to explore, I don't belong in this small town."

"Baby I don't even look at her in that way anymore. She is the mother to my children and nothing more. I can arrange to have them come over here instead." Would that be better?"

"I don't care if you look at her in that way or not. It looks bad and makes me feel *very* uncomfortable. And yes, it's much better if they come here. You're not allowed in that house anymore; meet her in a public place to pick them up."

"OK. We can arrange that."

It became the norm for him to get his kids for a couple of days while he was off from work, and they would visit with us over the weekend and on all his days off. I wasn't a kid person; I honestly was never fond of little kids, nor did I know how to entertain them. Holding a newborn baby had always bothered me because I just never knew how or wanted to deal with the "wobbly head syndrome" all newborns have. I have always been afraid that I'd hurt them by not properly holding and supporting their head. I never had to feed a baby or change a diaper in my life. I just never had to deal with a situation like this before. I honestly never really thought of having kids because I never wanted to mess up my body. I was selfish with my time and my life. I was afraid of delivery and thought childbirth was slimy and disgusting. Visions of gaining weight, being fat, and having my vagina ripped apart just didn't sit too well with me; it was something I never wanted to experience. I thought if I ever became pregnant that I'd be a horrible mom because I had no idea what to do with a baby.

When Curt, would get the kids, I would either leave and stay in the gym all day or go to my parents' house or be kind of distant and stay in our bedroom on the computer while they interacted in the living room. I didn't want to interfere, and I really didn't feel like bonding with the children because it reminded me of him being in a relationship and having sex with his wife. I knew he tried to give me more and more attention because he felt my tension with the situation. I honestly did think about breaking it off because it was way too much for me to take on. I wanted to leave because I just wasn't ready and felt I was too young for all this "be a stepmom to my kids" stuff. I was also very focused on my own life and my body because I had a national show coming up in less than ten weeks. I had no time to think about raising someone else's kids. He usually attended all my shows, but this fitness show was scheduled on the same week that he had his Air Force drill weekend.

The last few weeks leading up to the show, we were more intimate than ever. He couldn't keep his hands off me. We both knew we would be apart for at least five whole days, and this was a very long time for us because we had spent every single day together since we started dating.

Curt was such the protective/jealous type. The fact that he made me quit bartending showed his jealous side. He didn't want me working in that type of environment where other men could lust after me anymore.

Curt also knew that by me going to my bodybuilding competition in South Beach without him, I was going to be around lots of male energy and testosterone, and our relationship was already going downhill. I guess he felt the need to express his love even more physically during this time to make sure I was drained out and sexually satisfied before leaving. Satisfying me was never an issue for him. We never used protection and always resorted to using the withdrawal method for birth control because I knew my cycle like clockwork; I knew when I ovulated; I knew I was fertile on a couple of days I gave him the green light to ejaculate inside me.

After all this baby drama; seeing how fast his estranged wife bounced back to her petite pre-baby body and also seeing how loving and protective Curt was as a father, I began feeling nonchalant about becoming pregnant. I thought to myself, *I should have no problem getting my body back if I get pregnant. His wife got her body back pretty fast and she doesn't workout as much as I do, she's not even an athlete. Curt is so good with his boys without any help from me so he'll be good with our baby. If I get pregnant it will bring us closer and he trusts me knowing when I can and can't get pregnant so I'll set it up. I'll let him come in me while I'm ovulating, I probably won't get pregnant but it's worth a try for the sake of saving our relationship.*

I knew my cycle and was very in tuned with my body. I also believed that it was very hard for me to get pregnant, but I figured that if I did, it could possibly make me feel closer to him again, because I was feeling very distant from him and sad. I wanted to be connected to him in the same way his wife was, plus if I became a mom, it might make me a better stepmother.

A few weeks later, after strenuous training, dieting, and crazy sex, it was time for me to leave for Miami. I was on a tight budget since I didn't have my normal cash flow from bartending. Instead of flying like I was used to doing; it seemed more budget friendly for me to drive and not have to pay for transportation while being there. Curt gave me gas money and rented a car for me. I made it into a road trip with my best gym buddy and we split the bill. This was my first trip to South Beach ever, and I was really excited to go!

It was a long ten-hour ride, but when we finally got there and found our hotel, it looked amazing! I was very impressed when I pulled up and I couldn't believe the deal I got for ninety-nine dollars per night. The lobby looked absolutely grand and fabulous! Well, we got into the elevator, and it looked like a totally different hotel. It went from glamorous to ghetto really quickly! The rooms were terrible as well! There was a trail of ants walking up the bathroom wall, and there was a musty odor all through the room. The beautiful swimming pool that I saw online was empty and many of the tiles were missing out. The gym was filled with boxes and storage items and couldn't be used. It was *horrible* and looked nothing like it was beautifully portrayed online. It appeared to be going through renovations and I was ready to leave to go back home. Being on a tight budget, I couldn't afford a better hotel because the lowest rates started at two hundred ninety-nine dollars a night. I was grateful for having a place to rest my head and prayed that the spreads on our beds were clean and free from bed bugs.

Once we got settled in, I called to check in with Curt to tell him that we made it and also let him know of the poor condition of the hotel. My mind wasn't really focused on my show either; I began to feel separation anxiety from Curt and I wanted to hurry up and get through the weekend so that I could get back to him. The entire trip, we stayed connected via calls and text messages, and he had always been so very protective of me. When I told him about the quality of the hotel, he immediately turned into police protective mode and felt some kind of way thinking that maybe I was in a bad part of Miami. He wanted me to just stay in my room and not go around on a tour fearing for my safety. I obeyed him and didn't stray far from the hotel; I only left to get some food from the restaurant next door.

On the day of the show, I was much unfocused and just went through the motions of wanting to get it over with. I didn't even really try to do my hair. It rained that day and I had to walk to the pre-judging with no umbrella, my hair puffed out and looked horrible! I even felt a little sick and felt that my body wasn't lean enough despite all my efforts and discipline. My sense of smell was so keen, I could smell everything! The smell of all the oils and the different kinds of spray tan, hair-spray, and brush-on tan made me sick. I was actually quite nauseated. After the show was over, I finished nineteenth out of thirty or so competitors in my tall class and didn't care about my placement or motion myself to ask the judges what I needed to improve on. I was just ready to leave because I was feeling so sick and stressed about being so far away from Curt.

My gym buddy who came with me wanted to help me relax, so we went to a restaurant to celebrate me finishing the show and being able to eat a nice cheat meal. I usually order Bailey's Irish cream on the rocks or a red dessert wine because I love sweet drinks, but for some odd reason, I had no desire for alcohol or much cheat food. We ate our meal, and then went back to our hotel to pack for our long trip back home in the morning.

A few weeks later, I noticed my monthly cycle hadn't come the month of the show, nor did it come the current month I was in, which was December. At first I believed it was because of my low body-fat percentage prepping for my show, but when it didn't come the second month, I became very concerned. I was very sensitive to smell and couldn't stomach eating meat. I brought it up to Curt, and he told me to do a pregnancy test. I went ahead and bought a test from Walmart and then went to my parents' house to do it while Curt was at work.

Curt had no idea of the set up. I really wanted to be pregnant and allowed him to come inside me, knowing I was ovulating. I was so jealous of the fact that his wife had two children by him and feared that I could never have kids even if I wanted to. The possibility of being pregnant actually excited me because I truly believed that I would be one of those women who needed to go to a fertility specialist and try different methods to become pregnant when I was ready.

As I held the test in my hand, I crossed my fingers and prayed for a positive result, "Please God, let me be pregnant. It will make me feel closer to Curt. I'll do anything, I'll start going to church and pay my tithes and give offerings. Please!" After waiting five minutes for the results, I looked at the indicator, and it read 'PREGNANT'! This confirmed my uneasiness and sickness while I was at my show. There was a little life inside me and I was pregnant while I was on the stage!

Words can't describe how excited I am!
Until I write again,
Traci

CHAPTER 7

ABORTION
ULTIMATUM

Dear Diary,

I was so excited! I phoned Curt and told him what the test read, but he didn't seem too thrilled about it. He was working when I called and told me that he couldn't talk and had to get off the phone. He wasn't getting off until six in the morning, so I rushed to our apartment at about 5:45am to meet him there to talk. He seemed very cold and distant toward me. I understood the seriousness of the situation because he was still legally married and had just had a baby a few months before.

He gave me one option, and that option was abortion! I became very emotional because abortion was not allowed in my Christian family, and besides, how could I kill something as precious as my unborn baby if I couldn't even bear to kill an innocent deer with my car? We were talking about a little human life here. He was giving me what seemed to be an ultimatum of either keeping him as my man or keeping the baby. I began to think about it and knew everything would change if I did have the baby. I never really pictured myself being a mother, nor did I like the idea of losing my tight and fit physique. It was a very scary and semi-planned situation. I wanted this so bad, but I didn't expect that it would really happen, I had a huge decision to make.

After much persuasion, I folded to his pressure and let him set my appointment for the abortion. It was going to be done in Columbia at Planned Parenthood. When the day for the abortion came, I just couldn't go through with it. I could not physically drive myself there to do it alone.

Curt called and asked," How's it going? You ok?"

"I couldn't go, I'm still at home. There's no way I can drive myself to do that by myself."

He seemed a bit annoyed with me and then scheduled another appointment for the next week, this time in Charleston, and said he would take me himself to make sure it got handled.

On the scheduled day, I remember feeling sick, dizzy, and depressed all at the same time. It was a fifty-minute ride to the clinic. Halfway there,

I looked over at Curt, and told him that I wasn't going to go through with the abortion and that if it meant that we couldn't be together, so be it, I wouldn't be with him. I believed he was bluffing anyway, because how could your soulmate leave you for creating a love child? My thoughts were, *he treated his wife and kids so well and he knows this is his seed, there's no way he wouldn't be with me, we will be closer than ever now.*

Unexpectedly, he violently jerked the car over to the side of the road at the next exit nearly giving me whiplash. He dropped his head into his hands, paused, and said nothing for a moment.

He then lifted his head and asked, "Are you sure about this Traci? This is not a game; you're going to have to grow up. This is going to be a big responsibility and you're going to have to be accountable for another life other than your own. Are you sure you're ready for that, to give up your life for someone else's? You love your freedom and like to travel. Think of all your fitness shows, because that will come to an end. Everything you want to pursue will come to an end. Your life will belong to this baby and your life as you now know it will be over."

I confided in him that I could handle it and that I really had no choice but to handle it. Abortion has never been an option in my family. The mere fact that I was pregnant was a huge shock to my family because I was notorious for being very selfish and self-centered my entire life. I loved my freedom, I loved my workouts, and I was actually terrified. I hated the thought of gaining weight. It made me sick to my stomach thinking of gaining weight and seeing myself fat, but I believed that I'd be OK because I would have the love and support from Curt and my family. I wouldn't have to go through it alone.

I wanted to have a healthy and active pregnancy. Both my mom and older sister did very well and also didn't workout like I do. My sister was skinny and only gained fifteen lbs during her pregnancy and my mom who was very petite also only gained fifteen to twenty lbs for both me and my sister. I figured with this type of successful genetic track record of bounce back and small weight gain I'd be ok and not gain much weight. I needed to make sure everything was ok and healthy for me to stay active throughout my new pregnancy journey.

My new path of becoming a mom started pretty well. Curt and I went to the doctor to see exactly how far along my pregnancy was and to make sure it was healthy. As we walked in the building, I was immediately greeted by a nursing aid who took my morning pump classes at the gym.

"Hey Traci! Missed you this morning in class!"

"Yeah, I wasn't feelin' well. Who'd they get to sub for me?"

"Paul Mitchell. He wasn't you but he did a great job. I hope you feel better soon!"

"Thanks." After running into my student, I saw another gym member who took my spin classes who also worked at the doctor's office. She waved at me and I immediately began thinking to myself, *too many people know me here from the gym.* I waved back to her and continued to the women's care OB-GYN area. I approached the woman at the desk to sign in.

"Hi. I have an appointment to get an official pregnancy test to get approved for Medicaid and start my prenatal care here." I had to use Medicaid because I didn't have insurance anymore since leaving the restaurant and I was Curt's mistress and only our baby could go on his insurance after the delivery.

The front desk said," OK. You will be responsible for the bill until you get approved. After they approve you, you will be reimbursed or you can forward the bill to the insurance company."

I said, "So I can be billed and I don't have to make a payment to be seen today?

She said," Yes, we can bill you. Sign in and have a seat in the waiting area. Fill out this paperwork and we will call you in shortly."

I said, "OK." As I was signing my name in, a cute young nurse from the back walked up to the front desk and said," Hey Curt!"

Startled and hesitant he said," Oh... Hi Melissa."

Melissa, the nurse, said, "Long time stranger. How you been doing?"

Curt said, "I've been good."

There was a paused silence and it felt awkward. I looked at him wondering if he was going to introduce me to her and he didn't. I came out and said, "OH, he's doing really good." While rubbing my stomach I said," And we are expecting!"

Smiling with a surprised facial expression, she folded her arms and said, "OH wow! Congrats! And you are?"

Curt placed his arm round me and said, "This is my fiancé, Traci." I looked at him with a astonished face thinking, *Really? Your fiancé? Since when?*

Melissa said," Congrats to you two! Well, I have to get back to work. It was nice seeing you again Curt. I guess I'll be calling your fiancé in shortly." She then called the next patient in to be seen and they walked back into an exam room.

I grabbed the clipboard with the paperwork and we walked back to the seating area to sit down. I asked," Who the heck was that?" He told me that she was an old fling he used to deal with in nursing school. She knew that he was married when they messed around so that's why she was probably shocked and wondering if he got a divorce and why she didn't know about it."Well! You really weren't kidding when you told me that you got around! I won't be receiving my care here let's go!" I left the clipboard on the chair and we walked out without being seen by the doctor. I immediately told him that I'd find myself another doctor's office.

We lived in a small town and too many people knew me too personally from teaching classes at the gym and also this nurse, Melissa, who worked there was someone he dealt with before and I didn't feel comfortable, especially since I could tell she still fancied him. I was right about what I felt about her because she sent him a message over Facebook that evening saying how much she missed him and trying to find out details about his "divorce" to see if he was a "free man". She was totally disrespectful, not caring about my pregnancy. She messed with him while he was married, knowing that it was just a fling and nothing serious so she could care less about our new relationship. I had access to his Facebook and I told her not to message him ever again and deleted her from his friend's list and blocked her. I ended up getting a referral from my aunt to use a doctor in Lexington County that was forty minutes away and far from anyone who knew me and Curt personally.

It took almost two weeks to be seen but it was worth the wait. When we finally got to the new doctor's office, I feared all types of bad things would be wrong with my pregnancy because I was already ten weeks along and had been at five weeks when I did my show. I was taking all sorts of pills and supplements like pre-workouts, fat burners, water weight loss tablets, and had also consumed lots of alcohol on Thanksgiving prior to finding out about the pregnancy. I feared the worst to be wrong with my growing fetus from all that poison I dumped into my body. Despite consuming these unnatural products and alcohol, the doctor told me everything looked fine. She told me that after I get through my first trimester (12 weeks) and we knew the pregnancy was healthy, I would be given the OK to work out harder and continue teaching aerobics.

It's official! I'm going to be somebody's mommy!
Talk to you soon,
Traci

CHAPTER 8

THE BREAKUP

Dear Diary,

Curt was very supportive of our pregnancy together and was there for me through everything. I never got a ring but he was calling me his fiancé. He'd still continue to come to my job to watch me teach my classes and was very attentive to me, and we still made love. He really didn't want me to tell anyone about my pregnancy because I didn't look pregnant right away, but I had to tell my students at the gym because I'm pretty sure they would notice me not really going as hard as I used to. My doctor told me to keep a watch on my heart rate during my workouts and to slow down if it got higher than one hundred fifty. I'm sure they would notice that I wasn't pushing myself as hard, plus I was really excited about the pregnancy. I can't hold water when I'm excited, so I had to tell them. When he found out I told my students, he began to get distant again.

Once the word got out that I was pregnant, it spread viral, and Curt wasn't ready to tell his wife about the new baby. He did, however, want to be the one to tell her before she heard it from someone else. When he finally told her the news, it was devastating and she must have threatened him in some way. I wasn't present, but whatever she said to him was a game changer because he broke up with me not too long after that. He told me that we could no longer be together, that I had to move out, and he couldn't see a future with me anymore. It was on that day and at that moment that I knew my life was really changed forever. I became filled with anger; all I could see was red.

"I *hate* you! You're doing to me what you did to her! You're just going to leave me because I didn't abort? Who are you? You are not the man I fell in love with. He wouldn't leave me for creating a child out of love. I'm taking everything I brought here which is pretty much *every-thing*!" I furnished this place!"

I went off and broke the frame of our favorite photo that we took together. I destroyed any and everything I bought, dishes, paintings, chairs, I totally destroyed everything I could before he was able to grab me and then forced me to leave the apartment.

He said, "*Get* out! You're not the same woman I fell in love with, she wouldn't play me like this. You made the situation worse by getting pregnant and I know you set me up. You knew your cycle, you were jealous of my wife and you trapped me. You brought this upon yourself and now you can deal with it, *alone*. Get out of here *now*!"

"Fine! We don't need you!"

I packed up all my belongings and left, never to return again. From that moment on, I was alone. I had my parents' support, but I didn't have that emotional support and companionship I needed from my mate. Being pregnant is a very emotional time for a woman. I began to believe it was the karma I deserved from being involved with a married man. Now it was my turn to feel the burning heartache and experience what his wife possibly went through during her pregnancy because he left her to be with me. Karma is a bitch, and I wanted to die.

As depressing as everything was for me, I kept a smile on and continued to teach classes acting as if everything was ok and had my support group from my gym family and my parents. The management at the gym changed and they began to cut back on the amount of classes I taught because of my pregnancy even though I really needed the money at the time. I didn't have two jobs anymore, I had already stopped working as a bartender since Curt made me quit saying he would take care of me financially. Now I was stuck with earning a low income, I didn't make much money teaching aerobics and now I was making even less with fewer hours.

Though I needed the funds, I couldn't see myself go back to bartending being pregnant, and I didn't want to have to wear the uniform of a T-shirt and spandex shorts which is the requirement while pregnant. I doubt they'd take me back anyway because I really didn't leave in a good way. Before leaving the restaurant, I had become slack and missed shifts without calling in to let them know I wouldn't be there. I called out for the last time and they actually told me I was fired and that I didn't have to come in but I didn't care at the time because I had Curt's support financially, but now he was gone. I couldn't apply to be a flight attendant because that just wouldn't be a feasible move being pregnant. I applied for unemployment but it got rejected, I was in such a bad place financially and being pregnant made it worse. Every day was so lonely and sad, and it was becoming so hard to disguise my hurt and pain behind my cheerful smile every day; I was suffering. I had no one to blame but myself because I brought this upon myself and caused this pregnancy.

Visits to the doctor became so emotional, and I'd always break down and cry looking at all the happy, expecting couples. I felt like I was a statistic: a single black pregnant woman on Medicaid and WIC. I feared this would be my life, having to live off the government and collect food stamps and anything else I could get assistance for. I wanted to slit my wrists but couldn't bring myself to do it because the sight of my own blood makes me feel weak. I wanted to overdose on pills but felt too guilty having an innocent life growing inside me. I was so very depressed and suicidal and would go for long drives far away to park in dangerous, dark places, hoping someone would do the dirty work of taking my life. I would go for days without food or water, hoping to die from malnutrition and dehydration. Every kick I felt from my baby made me cry, I felt sorry for it because the father wanted nothing to with us. I had no desire to live, and I felt so alone, even though I had a baby moving around inside of me.

My mother noticed the depression and my lack of appetite. She forced me to eat and drink water and gave me pep talks and read Bible scriptures to me.

She read out from her bible, *"And he said unto me, My grace is sufficient for thee: for my strength is made perfect in weakness. Most gladly therefore will I rather glory in my infirmities, that the power of Christ may rest upon me. Therefore I take pleasure in infirmities, in reproaches, in necessities, in persecutions, in distresses for Christ sake: for when I am weak, then am I strong." -2 Corinthians 12:9-10*

"Mom, I just want to be alone, I want to die."

"The devil is a *liar* and I *rebuke* that spirit of depression and suicide from your body! I *plead* the blood of Jesus over your life and Curt's life. Traci this is when you really need to speak to the Lord. You need to pray and ask God for forgiveness and get yourself back in church."

"Mom please. You'll never understand what this feels like because you got pregnant in wedlock. I just really want to be left alone."

My mom is a very religious and spirit filled Christian woman, she told me that I needed to give my life over to Jesus, but I didn't want to hear her. She had no idea how I felt because she planned her pregnancies after she got married to my father and had his support physically and financially from the start. She did things the right way and never had to worry about money or my dad's support. He was always there and a great provider for us. She had no idea the pain I felt being pregnant and alone.

I finally listened to her and went to church for a couple Sundays and it felt good to be around loving people, but then it didn't last too long. I just missed Curt too much and seeing happy couples in the church with families made me feel depressed again. Curt was my best friend, and I had no friends or anybody else to talk to. All the girls I grew up with were back in New York, and I had never really made any true close friends in South Carolina that I could really share all my deep emotions and pain with. I had my gym friends and they helped me as much as they could, they even threw me a baby shower at the gym and I was so appreciative because I didn't have anyone else to do it. A baby shower was supposed to be a happy time and I played the part but I was dying inside. I didn't want to let them know too much about my personal life and I just couldn't shake the hurt and pain in my heart; I suffered in silence. I'd fall right back into a deep depression after I was alone again; my bed became my sanctuary.

Ready to die,
Traci

CHAPTER 9

LOVE OR MONEY?

Dear Diary,

I just wanted Curt, my soul mate, back. He was so different from any guy I'd ever dated. He was the only man capable and who I allowed to get me pregnant. I'd had three serious and monogamous relationships before Curt, never having one pregnancy scare. I truly believed that it would take a fertility specialist or a miracle to ever conceive a child. This is why Curt is near and dear to me; the universe/God allowed him to procreate with me. He is my soul mate, and it took my life force away when he broke up with me. He took my spirit and desire to live away. The only thing that was alive was my growing baby inside of me. I couldn't keep the pain I felt a secret anymore and would lay in bed and began to make depressing posts over social media to vent my feelings to the world.

"All I do is give my heart and it always gets burned. What ever happened to loyalty? All men suck. I just don't want to live anymore. I wonder if my baby can feel my emotional pain."

When I would make sad posts like these, a few of my gym buddies and students tried to cheer me up. One time, Mrs. Red Cross, a great friend from the gym who attended my aerobics classes regularly, texted me and told me to get up and get out of bed and come over to her house for breakfast. I really didn't want to go, but I knew that I needed to get out of the house to feel better, plus she told me that if I didn't get up that she would come to my parent's house to get me up. She texted me her address and It took me a long time to get ready because It was hard trying to find clothes that fit since I refused to buy maternity clothes. A friend of mine, Michelle, from the gym, told me to put a rubber band in my jeans to expand the waistline and it worked! I then put on a T-shirt and then headed out. I put her address into my phone's MapQuest and it brought me to a really nice part of town I had never seen before. My parents lived in a pretty nice middle class neighborhood next to a lake but her neighborhood looked way more exclusive. All the houses were enormous and had huge driveways with in-ground swimming pools. I finally found her house and rang the doorbell. She opened the door and I was greeted with a warm hug. I really needed it.

She made me grits, eggs, toast, and turkey bacon with orange juice and fresh fruit. I passed on the turkey bacon because I was vegan/vegetarian at the time. Yes, I had a vegetarian pregnancy! The smell and taste of real meat just made me sick to my stomach, and I was trying my best not to gain too much weight, but it seemed that no matter how healthy and clean I ate, nor how much working out I did, the pounds kept packing on heavily week after week. Mrs. Red Cross told me how great I looked despite being so far along. I was over six months pregnant at that time.

She tried to comfort me and told me about her struggles when she first got pregnant by her husband. He's an ER surgeon now, and they became pregnant while he was still in his residency. She told me all about their struggles emotionally and financially because they were so young and just starting out, but they had made it through the trials and have a loving and successful marriage. I was looking around at her beautiful home as she talked to me. It was fabulous, and she had an amazing kitchen, where we were eating breakfast. She could tell I was in awe of her home so she gave me a tour and showed me her home gym and she had a huge library of home workout DVDs. They had two young children; she was the perfect prototype of a fit and healthy housewife. She was an educated woman with multiple degrees but didn't have to work because her husband was a surgeon and had an amazing income. She was very well kept, so fit and pretty, and she got styled by best and most expensive master hair stylist in town daily; gorgeous hair and fingernails looking amazing every day.

I must admit, I was a bit jealous and envious of her lifestyle! I was very happy for her though because she deserved it all and was living her happy fairy tale life with her king. She had an amazing spirit, and she was always a joy to have in my 5:00 a.m. classes. She brought amazing energy into my early morning sweat sessions. There's always that vibrant gym member who hypes the rest of the class up when they walk into the room, and she was one of them!

"Traci, you're still young and you have a lot going for you. The way you teach classes is like your calling and ministry. You're very talented and inspire so many of us to want to be fit. I'm sure Curt will come around after your baby is born. Just give it some time. He is probably missing you too."

"He ignores me, I just feel that this is my karma because he's lawfully married. This isn't how I planned my life to be Mrs. Red Cross. I'm a pregnant mistress soon to be a single mom on government assistance. My story isn't turning out to be too good, it's so depressing. I wish I was happy and had joy like you."

"Traci, just pray, and keep coming to church, the Lord will see you through. Remember that God never puts more on us than we can bear. You will pull through this like a champ. I believe that you're even strong enough mentally and physically to deliver that baby without an epidural!"

"Well, I don't know about all that. I may try to do it natural just to prove to Curt, that I really love him and would go through the pain for him."

Mrs. Red Cross gave me life and made me feel so much better. She even told me how she went all natural with her second pregnancy and didn't get an epidural. That's what I wanted to do with my pregnancy as well, have a natural childbirth with no medicine. I wanted to show Curt how much I loved him and that I would go through the pain out of love.

I wished my story was like Mrs. Red Cross's story; she had love and success. I wanted that happy fairytale ending with my king, but my story wasn't going so well. Seeing her happiness and success put me back to thinking about my ex, the ER doctor, because he was very financially secure. It made me want to reach back out to him to see if maybe he could rescue me from my nightmare and whether we could possibly rekindle where we left off. I knew Mr. ER Doctor still loved me, and I just wanted to get the hell out of Dodge so I wouldn't have to see Curt or his wife and kids ever again.

After I left Mrs. Red Cross's house, I went ahead and sent a text in all caps to my ex, Dr. Grey. "HEY STRANGER! JUST THINKING OF YOU!" To my surprise he responded immediately, "Hi gorgeous!" Then he poured his heart out to me about how much he missed me and apologized for his infidelity. I was so happy he was missing me and I told him

I missed him as well. However, I didn't tell him about my pregnancy yet. He was working at a hospital in Texas and wouldn't be back until the next week so I agreed to meet him at a nearby restaurant the following week when he returned.

I arrived at the restaurant before him and got us a table near the back for privacy. I sat facing the door so that I could see when he arrived, I was so nervous because I didn't know how he would react to the news of my pregnancy. He walked in and smiled at me as he approached the table. I smiled back and then stood up so he could see my body. He was shocked when he saw my baby bump.

"Woah! You're pregnant! I see you've been a very busy lady. So who's the lucky guy?"

"Im not happy Dr. Grey, I'm miserable and the father has left me to deal with this pregnancy alone! He left me because I wouldn't abort."

I poured my heart out to him and began to cry as we interlocked our hands. He then embraced me in a hug and told me that everything would be ok. I felt a warmth and comfort being in his presence again, even after knowing about his fiancé in Barbados and his other fling in Atlanta. After I calmed down, I asked him about them and the status of their relationships, and he told me that he'd ended it with the Bajan girl because he'd found out she was a gold digger and using him and other men to get married just so that she could get to the United States. I then asked about the Pro cheerleader and he said that she was a gold digger too.

Laughing I said, "Well that's what you get! You need to stay away from the young girls, they only want money. Me on the other hand, I'm young, but I only want to be loved. Material things are nice but genuine love is priceless. You really hurt me Edward." I shared my story about how I met Curt, how I became pregnant nearly seven months along already. He was very receptive and open to me.

He said, "What kind of man would leave a woman because she's pregnant with his child? He's a coward. I would've loved for you to carry my child. You're going to make an amazing mother. He must be crazy."

I said, "It's my fault Dr. Grey, I got pregnant on purpose because I was jealous that his wife had two kids with him. He left his wife while she was pregnant too! I guess I deserve this, I should have known better than to become involved with a married man who had the heart to leave his pregnant wife. History repeats itself and I deserve to feel this pain."

My baby began to kick and I placed my hand on my stomach.

"He's kicking the heck out of me right now! I'm so amazed at how there's a little human life growing inside me, it's like a miracle, it's a beautiful thing but yet I'm so sad."

Dr. Grey asked if he could feel the kicks and he placed his hand on my stomach. He told me that he wanted to start over again and that we could raise my child together. He told me that I was glowing and was even more attractive to him being pregnant.

"I'm ready to settle down. I really had love with you and all these women I date are only after money. You are truly one of a kind and I now know your love was real. I was happiest when we were together, let's start over again. I'll take care of you if you take care of me."

He spoke of us moving to Florida to begin our new life together and how he was ready to settle down. He wanted to find his dream home close to the ocean (Cancers love water), and he was ready to be married. As I listened to him, I began to get sad again. As dreamy and secure as the future seemed to be with Dr. Grey, I began to think about Curt and my growing baby. I was such an emotional wreck. I began to cry again.

Deep down I really didn't want to be with Dr. Grey because the love I once had for him wasn't the same love anymore. His timing was so off because I wanted to be with him before I found out about his cheating ways. I did still care for him as a friend, but it wasn't the way it used to be because he hurt me so badly. The romance just wasn't there anymore, my feelings weren't strong enough to want to marry him and be with him for the rest of my life; I didn't want to pretend.

Money and material things couldn't buy my heart. I wanted to feel true joy and passion, and it wasn't there. Once my heart is broken, it's just like a shattered bone and impossible to piece back together. I could never feel that same passion I felt when we first met. I didn't want to end up being one of those women who have it all—money, cars, beautiful homes, exotic trips—but no love between partners. Having true unconditional love is wealth, and without it there is no meaning to life, love can't be one sided, it needs to flow. Everyone searches for this type of love in their lifetime; it's what completes us as humans and keeps our species alive. A true soul mate/twin-flame union is what we were made for (I'll explain this later in the book). We ended dinner, and he immediately wanted me to come back to be with him, but I told him I had to really think on it. He gave me a kiss and a hug and let me go on my way.

I don't want material things, I just want love.
Sincerely,
Traci

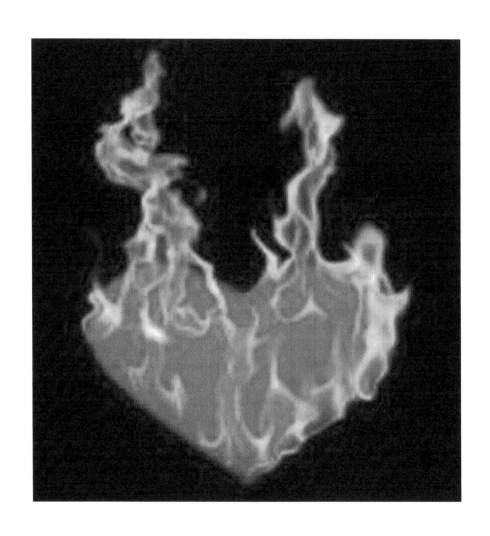

CHAPTER 10

RAGE

Dear Diary,

After visiting with my ex, I couldn't help but wonder what Curt, was up to. Did he get back with his wife? Was he dating someone new? It just bothered me because we were no longer speaking. I had deleted him from my Facebook page and was unable to keep up with what he was doing or posting on his social media. I reached out to our mutual friends to see what type of posts he was making. Most of his friends wouldn't share any of his information with me. I guess they were trying to protect him and didn't want to violate their friendship. The ones I asked were actually a part of his fraternity, so they probably didn't want to betray their brotherhood. I did however get a mutual female friend to get screenshots of his timeline wall and send them to me.

To my surprise it seemed as if he was very happy and enjoying his summer and his freedom from me. In one status, he was going on about how good all the ladies were looking in their revealing summer attire, and he was openly flirting with one of his sorority sisters who we both knew had a crush on him. She was all over his page, commenting and liking his pics and also very active on all his statuses. I immediately assumed they were messing around with one another because she wasn't on his page like that before our breakup.

I wrote a long private Facebook message explaining to her why she should stop messing with him; how many kids he had; that he was still married with a newborn from his wife and that he also had a baby on the way with me. She hit me back and said they were not messing around and also that she knew about me and actually was happy that we split up because she was his friend long before I came into the picture. She didn't like how distant he became to her once we started dating and also said that she would have his back no matter what his situation was. Whether she was messing with him or not, I didn't like her response because she was happy we were no longer together and it was like she was saying that she was always going to be in his life even if I wasn't. This made me livid!

The fact that this girl seemed to have a better relationship with Curt and could communicate with my man whenever she wanted to and could possibly be screwing around with him really ticked me off. I wanted to fight her! Forget hair grabbing and scratching faces like most chicks do when they fight, If she was in front of me I swear I would have punched her so hard in her pretty little nose to break it, game over! My emotions were on fire! It was late in the evening, and I didn't want to wait until morning to confront Curt, about the situation. I knew he wouldn't answer his phone or text messages, so after having a conversation with myself about whether or not I should pay him a visit (I spoke to myself a lot, being pregnant can make you a little crazy in the head sometimes), I made an executive decision to drive to his town house to see if he was home to get some answers from him.

Driving was very difficult for me because my SUV needed repairs that I couldn't afford to get at the time since I didn't have the money coming in. Since I was staying with my parents, I had to resort to driving my father's '89 Corvette, which was a cute and sexy little red sports car, but it was not pregnancy friendly. It was a car that you only drive around for show and was a two-seater; it was such a struggle to get in and out of since it was so very low to the ground. I'm very tall, and my big pregnant belly and long legs made it very hard to drive. I also felt a strain in my stomach and uterus when I lifted myself out. It was all I had, so I dealt with it.

When I got to his place, both his personal car and patrol car were parked in his driveway, so I knew he was inside. I wanted to see if he'd answer his phone, so I called before going to knock on his door. He didn't answer. I then walked up to the door and began to knock. He opened the door and appeared to have been sleeping. I walked inside and looked around to see if I could find any evidence or traces of another woman being there. I just knew he had to revert back to his Playboy ways; I walked up to his room and the upstairs bathroom searching for anything that wasn't mine. I found nothing, I then took out my phone to show him the Facebook messages exchanged between me and his "friend" on my phone and questioned about them messing around. He laughed and said no, that she was just a friend. I didn't believe him because she wasn't an ugly girl, she was his sorority sister, an AKA (Alpha Kappa Alpha) and this sorority is known for only having beautiful women as members, and she was very single and I knew she liked him and he obviously had to be attracted to her as well. I was feeling so insecure and didn't believe him.

I began to cry and told him how lonely I had been without him and that I really needed him. I was so jealous that someone else could get his energy and attention and I couldn't. I poured my heart out. Curt was my only best friend, and I had nobody else. I even told him that I had been so horny for weeks and really needed to feel his love. I was the most insecure I had been in my entire life! I felt very fat and very ugly.

I moved in to give him a hug, and he allowed it. I began to squeeze him tightly, and he lifted his arms to hug me back. We then began to kiss, and he began to feel up on my body. He ran his hands up my back and then around to my pregnant belly. I was wearing a sundress because it was the only thing I could wear comfortably, and he then pulled down my straps. My breasts were very tender and swollen. I wasn't producing milk yet, but they were much larger than they were pre-pregnancy. He grabbed them and began to caress them. I closed my eyes and just wanted to cherish the moment because I longed to feel him touch me. I'd been so lonely and felt so unloved. I was finally getting the attention I wanted and needed from him!

Curt always knew exactly how to please me and was always so in tune with my body. As he caressed my pregnancy breasts, he began to lick around my enlarged and freakishly darker areolas (another weird side effect from being pregnant). My breasts have always been my sensitive spot, but due to the pregnancy, they were even more sensitive than ever. I felt borderline pain and pleasure as he kissed on them and it turned me on so much.

He then lifted my dress, removed my panties, backed me up to his couch, and laid me down. I couldn't lay directly on my back because I felt pain and pressure in my uterus, so I turned onto my left side, which was more comfortable for me. He slid my dress off completely, and he was about to make love to me when I noticed his erection was going away and was too soft to penetrate inside me. I immediately began to feel insecure because I was very uncomfortable with my enlarged pregnant body; he had never lost an erection with me before. I was always able to please him every time we made love. I was always able to make him climax more than once when we'd make love. There was always more than just a physical connection between us. We had a spiritual bond as well, but it all felt so physical this time, no power. My face had even changed—my nose was larger—and I just felt so ugly and undesirable. I wasn't my normal, confident self, and I could tell he wasn't with me mentally.

I asked him what was wrong, and he told me that he just had a lot on his mind and apologized to me. I really wanted to please him so that he wouldn't have to go somewhere else to be satisfied. It would break my heart if he was with someone else.

As I began to put my dress back on, I said, "It's me, isn't it? I don't turn you on. I'm really fat and probably the biggest woman you've ever been with. Have you ever been with a woman as tall and big as I am now? I weigh more than you!" The insecurities from my relationship with Dr. Grey began to haunt me again. Curt too may have a preference for petite women; his estranged wife was short and barely over a hundred pounds pre-pregnancy.

He said, "No. It's not you. I'm just under a lot of stress. I think you should go back home. I have to get up early in the morning for work."

I said, "OK, just promise me that you'll come with me to my next doctor's appointment so I won't be alone?" He asked when it was, and I told him, "The day after tomorrow, and you should be off work on that day."

He said he would try to make it and to send him a reminder about it. I then left and went back home, feeling more depressed than ever. The tears couldn't be held back. He wasn't attracted to me anymore!

I waited and anticipated a call or text from him the next day and got nothing. The entire day went by without a word. I called, then texted, and still nothing. The next day came, but I didn't hear from him again. I reminded him about my doctor's appointment and still got no response.

I began to get worried that maybe something bad happened to him. Being a state trooper it's never guaranteed that he would make it home safely after every shift. There was a bad accident where a trooper got struck by a speeding car while working a wreck on the interstate and

I thought it was Curt. I found out it was another trooper but I was still apprehensive about him and his safety. I drove by his place, and to my surprise, he wasn't at home. He left and didn't say a word to me. He seemed to have no concern about me and my pregnancy. I blew up his phone with threatening text messages about filing for child support and moving away to get married to someone else.

Silence was his answer, and the silence was deadly. My depression turned into rage! I was pregnant, and he was ignoring me? What if this was an emergency? What if I was dying? He wasn't at home, and it was late at night, which made me assume that he was with somebody else, probably his sorority sister. I wasn't pleasing him, so he must've been getting pleasure from somewhere else. Curt's sex drive was crazy, he always wanted sex, losing an erection with me was a big deal. I just knew he couldn't go but for so long without having intimacy. I went into my bag and got a piece of paper and wrote the nastiest letter I could think to write and left it on his door:

Dear Curt,

I hate you. I hope you catch a disease where your dick shrivels up and falls off. I hope you fuck somebody that makes you so sick that you can never be with anybody else again. You are a monster. You are terrible. How can you do this to me, your soul mate? Karma is going to come back and bite you in the ass, and when it does, I probably won't be around to see it because I am going to leave. You are the scum of the earth. You are a nightmare; your name should be Freddy Fucking Krueger because you are my nightmare. I wish all the deadbeat and slut-bag men could get rounded up, placed on a huge rocket, and blasted out into space, far away from this planet! You're irresponsible, and if you're out dipping into some other dumb bitch and you get her pregnant, you're going to have another baby on the way, and then what? You've turned me into a statistic and brought me down to your level. You're a typical black man with multiple baby mothers. I should've gotten pregnant by a white man. I bet a white man would've treated me better than you and made me feel loved. I'm carrying your child, and I've been so depressed and stressed out. I was told the baby can feel my emotions and pain! You're so ignorant, and I hate you. I never want to see you again. You never cared about me! All you do is play women! I will deliver this baby alone, without you. I don't need you in my life. Just know that I am going to hit you up for child support and everything that I can get from you. You're going to pay for this. You're not going to get away. You are going to pay. I never wish bad fortune on people but when I heard that a state trooper got struck by a speeding car while working a wreck, I was praying to God that it was you! I wish it was you who got hit while you were working and not Howard. I thank God he's ok and he wasn't the one who deserved to get hit; *you* were. He's a good man who loves and takes care of his family, He'd never do this to Latoya because he really loves her and you never loved me! I was just convenient ass for you. You're a deadbeat, cheating-ass, no good slutbag! I wish it was you lying in the hospital right now because you need to be put in your place and slowed down. You didn't get hit but karma will find you; you will be dealt with eventually!

Enjoy your night, ASSHOLE!
Traci

I waited a couple of days to see if he would text me or call me but I got nothing. He never responded; he never called. I left it alone for a few days, trying to just focus on myself and the baby. I tried to forget about him like he obviously forgot about me, but while watching TV, my family saw him on a commercial.

My mom yelled out, "Traci! Come here quick! Isn't this Curt?"

"Oh my God! Yes it's him! He looks great! Ugh! I hate him mom! I'm mad they chose him, this is going to go straight to his head. He's so arrogant and doesn't deserve this type of attention and shine!"

"Traci, hate is such a strong word. Just say you don't like his ways right now. God is working with that young man, you don't know what he's going through and I will continue to pray for you both."

"I'm just mad; can you turn it to another channel? I'm sure it will come on again, I don't want to see it."

They chose him to be the face of the highway patrol! Everywhere I went people were talking about him being on the TV and apparently he had a billboard on the interstate too; you couldn't escape it, he was everywhere. The state was running the commercial into the ground playing it over and over again on different stations. He was the star of the state's DUI commercial, and this made me even more upset because I didn't really want to see him doing well! I wished bad fortune on his life but instead of receiving bad fortune, he was being blessed and his career was taking off while my life was going down. It seemed he was just living life to the fullest and moving on without me! I was so sure he was getting a lot of attention from being on a billboard and the TV—especially from women. He was very recognizable and looked really great in the commercial, I felt so sure that even more women would be throwing themselves at him when trying to get out of citations. I was jealous of him and there was nothing I could do about it; he was ignoring me. I got desperate and texted the wife of another trooper to find out what his schedule was so that I could be sure to catch him as soon as he got off his shift. I got the information, and then I waited for him to get off work so that I could see him in person.

He must have gotten off work early that day because when I got to his house in the morning, at the time he should've been getting off from work, he was already gone, and the patrol car was left in his driveway. That was the final straw! I went to the Dollar General Store up the road and bought some eggs and shaving cream. I was going to jack up his car. I wanted to bust out all the windows and flatten the tires!

Being that this was not his personal vehicle and that it belonged to the state, I knew I could be facing a felony charge if someone saw me or if he reported me, but I didn't care. He would have to send me to jail or to a mental hospital because I was so angry and crazy. I threw the entire carton of eggs on his car, cursing him, and then wrote the words DEADBEAT and CHEATER on the front driver side window with shaving cream. I then took a screw driver out my dad's tool box in the Corvette to let the air out of his tires. It was taking too long to deflate without causing damage so I found some nails in the same box and wedged them between the ground and his back tires so that when he'd reverse, it'd puncture his tires causing a slow leak. I didn't want to cause permanent damage, because it was the state's vehicle, but just enough to slow him down and get his attention. It took me less than ten minutes, then I got back in the Vette and drove off feeling such a rush; it felt so good! There was no way that he could ignore that. He was going to have to say something and confront me about it.

This was something totally out of character for me because I had never acted that way before in my entire life. I can normally walk away from a situation, but this was completely different, and I couldn't just walk away. I couldn't just escape. I couldn't just jump on an airplane to become a flight attendant and leave the country. I now had the responsibility of a child who might end up looking like this father that I hated so bad. I was stuck, this was a nightmare and felt like a prison sentence; my body no longer belonged to me, it belonged to Curt's seed.

I finally got a text message from him: "Are you out of your mind? Do I need to get a restraining order on you? You've desecrated a government vehicle, and you can go to jail for this!" I told him that I didn't care and that he could come to lock me up himself. I asked what he'd been doing with his time he obviously wasn't spending it with me. He told me not to worry about it and just to take care of myself. I asked him if I could come over to see him, but he said no. Of course, since I knew he was at home, I took my pregnant self over to see him anyway.

As I was pulling up, the Corvette shut off. I tried to crank it back up, but it was just dead and the engine wouldn't turnover. It was raining very hard outside and he noticed me through his living room window struggling trying to get the car started, and he came outside. He asked what I was doing in front of his place. I told him I just wanted to see him and that the car broke down. I asked him if he could help me get it started and if I could come inside out of the rain, and he said, "No, I'll call a tow truck to come help you." He didn't even help me or invite me in out of the bad weather; he had somebody else come tow my car. Not only was my car towed, but Curt made the tow service bring me home, when he could have driven me in his personal car. What man would allow a woman who is carrying his child to stay out in the pouring rain and to ride home with a weird and complete stranger?

I felt so fat, ugly, and unattractive! I'd never felt such rejection before in my life. I'd been so good at protecting myself from this type of pain my entire life. Everyone thought so highly of Curt. Even this tow truck driver who drove me home was going on raving about how they call Curt "Hollywood" because he does the state's highway patrol commercials and how he's the sharpest trooper he's ever seen. This driver knew Curt, because he usually tows the cars away from the wrecks that he worked. I got annoyed and wanted him to shut up praising Curt. I sure did let him know what a deadbeat he was and that he wasn't all that great of a father and shouldn't be commended for anything.

I was filled with so much hurt and anger that I wanted to get revenge! I was pregnant with his baby and he left me to deal with it alone while he lived his life and had fun like I never existed? If I died he probably wouldn't even care because he'd have nothing to worry about anymore. I wasn't going to give him that satisfaction. No longer feeling depressed or suicidal, I felt determined to get his attention and began to plot my plan for after I had my baby. I wanted to do something that he could never forget, then leave him behind and marry my ex.

I began to research online how I could get my body back fast. I saw Deon Sander's wife (Pilar, I believe her name was) bounce back really fast and had a ripped six pack in only six months after having her baby, she was on an infomercial for an ab machine. I've seen so many women in the fitness industry who were older than me, with several kids, bounce back fast within five and six months from giving birth; even Curt's wife dropped her baby weight super-fast so I needed to find out what did I need to know; what did I need to do to get my body back fast? There had to be a scientific approach to it! There was so much information but none of what I was looking for to help me do what I wanted do. Then I came across something that spoke about the relaxin hormone and how it causes a woman's joints and muscles to relax and expand, allowing room to carry a baby. I also read that this hormone stays present as long as you're a breastfeeding mom, for up to eight to ten weeks. I immediately thought to myself, *Oh my Goodness! I can mold myself back into shape faster and even smaller than I was before if I wear shapewear!* More information I discovered was that pregnant women produce high levels HCG and it stays present for a week or two after giving birth. I also read that breastfeeding burned over five hundred calories per day. I became obsessed with this information and planned on using it as my ammunition to fight the fat away. I kept reading and researching different things because I couldn't stay stuck being over two hundred pounds.

One late night, apparently my son was having a kick-boxing match with my bladder and I was awakened having to pee. I got up to use the bathroom and then had a chocolate sugar craving, I guess my baby was awake and hungry. I decided to make a thick chocolate protein shake with graham crackers, bananas, strawberries, peanut butter, and topped it off with whipped cream. I turned my TV on to watch while I indulge my treat, then I began to get sleepy again. While sleepiness was all over me and my eyes began to close, I saw an infomercial for a workout DVD that claimed to be America's hardest workout.

"You want a ripped body with abs? Well you don't need an expensive gym membership to get one. Just a DVD player and enough space for a puddle of sweat. Get off that couch and earn it! I challenge you! I want you to *Dig Deeper!*"

I immediately caught a second wind and became overtaken by what I saw. I wanted to get up right then and there and workout! Along with all the research I had done, the infomercial gave me even more hope of getting myself back to pre-pregnancy weight. I'm not one who likes to lift heavy believing that internal/callisthenic strength is healthier and looks better than bulky muscle tone. I loved the idea of doing max interval training using only my body weight. The workouts looked very intense like something I'd love to put my body through once I was free from the handicap of pregnancy. Seeing all the sweaty, ripped, and fatigued bodies made me want to go ahead and place an order for it. I became like a ticking time bomb ready to explode and get my bombshell physique back. I was so filled with hatred and animosity towards Curt, ready to begin intense training *immediately.*

I was focused and began to nest in preparation for my baby's arrival. My nesting wasn't the normal nesting of putting together a nursery, baby proofing, and cleaning the entire house; no, my nesting consisted of cleaning out the garage and turning it into a home gym. I told my parents I wanted to turn their garage into my workout space for after my delivery since I wouldn't be going to the gym. Their garage was a huge project because it was filled with so much storage from the move from New York years ago, it was infested with so many webs that had creepy spiders and it freaked me out but it had to get cleaned out for me to work out; it took days to clear it out completely. I think we used over three cans of bug spray, there are so many spiders in the south and I'm terrified of them, but I was determined to have my workout space. Once it was cleared, we put a TV and DVD player in, along with some light free weights, a step bench, a spin bike, and a sound system. I was all set ready to go!

I also ordered three different sizes of waist cinchers so that I could begin to waist train as soon as I had my baby (I learned about waist cincher training from my gym momma and also read that Brazilian woman used *fajas* to get their banging bodies back after having their kids). I had my fitness plan all ready to get my body back fast and get Curt's attention by being so freaking hot that whatever chick he ended up with would really question why he left me (from a physical point of view). I wanted to look good really quickly after having my baby. I had my plan all sorted out. 1) Get fit fast. 2) File for child support. 3) Skip town with my ex to become a privileged Doctor's wife and pursue my fitness career.

Screw Curt! I'm ready to get my life back together.
Sincerely,
Traci

CHAPTER 11

THE DELIVERY

Dear Diary,

I was so ready to get back into the game. He was over me, and I was ready to get over him. It was easier for him to forget about me because I wasn't my normal sexy and fit self, I was an angry pregnant woman who was plotting and seeking revenge on him. We stopped communicating completely but I still continued to put nails in the tires of both his cars without him knowing it was me every time I passed by his house and saw he wasn't home.

Prior to my pregnancy, I was one hundred forty-five pounds at my fitness show. By the time I was eight months pregnant, I was already two hundred pounds! Every doctor visit I went to, the scale just kept going up, no matter how clean I ate or how much cardio and strength training I did. I worked out for at least two hours a day trying not to gain weight, but I did anyway. The massive weight gain just wasn't making any sense to me! My doctor told me that I was pretty tall and that my body was going to gain whatever weight it needed to gain in order to sustain a healthy pregnancy.

"Ok, dear, step on the scale."

"Can I stand on it backwards? I'll freak out if I see it over two hundred pounds."

"Yes that's fine."

"No tell me, I want to know, it'll be my motivation."

"OK. You're two hundred three pounds."

"Oh my God! No way! Dr. Skinner this is just crazy! My mom and sister didn't gain much weight and they ate everything in sight with no type of workouts. I'm busting my tail and eating healthy! This just isn't fair!"

"You can never compare pregnancies like that because every woman's body handles it differently. You're also six foot tall so you need the extra weight. For your height you actually started your pregnancy underweight. Aren't you a trainer? I'm sure it won't stick. Don't worry yourself, you're entering the home stretch and will see your son soon. When you see his face it will all be worth it."

"Yea, I was at my fitness competition weight when I got pregnant so I guess my body just kept shooting up weight from there for being calorie stricken. I'm praying my son doesn't look like his dad because I hate him."

"Well, you're doing very well, heartbeat sounds wonderful, those workouts are great for his little heart. He'll probably be athletic just like his mom!"

"Yea, he has no choice but to be an athlete. It runs in our blood and we have several professional athletes in the family. Do you follow pro football?"

"No, not too much. I do watch the Super bowl though."

"Oh ok, well I have a cousin who plays for the Atlanta Falcons and one who is retired from the Jets."

"That's cool, well maybe you've got a little football star in there!"

"Hope so! I'm just ready to push him out and get my body back; I'm so over being this big. I hate not having control over my body."

I taught until a week out from my delivery. If it were up to me, I'd teach until my delivery date. I actually got kicked out of the gym from teaching my scheduled water aerobics class. The new aquatics manager at the time seriously discriminated on me for being pregnant. He unplugged my iPod from the sound system as I began to play my warm up music and he handed it to me telling me that I needed to leave and that he had someone else to teach my class for me. He did it in a very rude manor that upset the class as well. This happened to be the largest aqua class I had ever had. There were over sixty bodies in attendance, a bunch were pregnant women who were inspired by my dedication to fitness throughout my pregnancy, and there were many spectators who just liked to sit and watch me teach the class from the bleachers and loved the old school music I used.

This manager (who happened to be younger than me) took it upon himself to decide that I was too far along to teach anymore classes. He was new to the gym and had no idea of who I was or the history I had there. He had no clue that I helped to build a strong group fitness program at the facility from the time the doors were opened for business and the paint was still wet on the walls. When he began working there as one of the managers, the impression he gave me when we first met was of disgust, he didn't seem too thrilled to have me teaching classes because I was pregnant, overweight, and not the ideal instructor he was probably used to seeing. I didn't like his energy and knew it'd be a matter of time before we bumped heads. I do admit that I was quite huge and looked as if I could go into labor at any moment but that was none of his business. After this disrespect and unprofessionalism, I told him that I was going to file a discrimination charge against him and I grabbed my belongings and left out. Half the class and all the spectators left out as well and many canceled their gym memberships because they were upset about what transpired and how it was handled.

I sat in my car in the parking lot crying with my head on the steering wheel," *God!* What else is going to happen to me? I'm *fat*, ugly, pregnant and alone and now my passion has been taken away from me! They don't care about me! What *else* is left? Why is this happening? There has to be something better that's going to come for me because I can't imagine getting any lower than this. I'm broke; I have nothing to offer my son. I tried to stay as fit as possible throughout this entire pregnancy. I'm such a *failure!*" Suddenly there was a knock on my window. It was Yolanda, an avid gym member who took all my classes and also an awesome support to me throughout my pregnancy.

"Girl, what are you doing in here? Why aren't you teaching your class? I was on my way in."

Sniffling and wiping the tears off my face I said, "They kicked me out because they claim I'm too far along in my pregnancy. Half the class left out and they have a lifeguard teaching the class who isn't even certified to instruct. I'm never coming back here again, I'm done!"

Yolanda said, "I knew it was a matter of time before this happened. They were talking about how much you've been training and were concerned for the health of both you and your baby. But only you know yourself and your limits. All I can say is just let me know where you will be teaching when you're ready to come back off maternity and I will be there. You should look into Tony and Maria's place because they're looking for instructors at their gym. I'm going to go home for a run since you're not teaching tonight, take care of yourself, Traci, wipe those tears and keep your head up. You're going to be just fine."

"Thanks Yolanda, I'll definitely check them out. I just can't believe what happened tonight. Well, I'll see you around. I'm gonna try to get this baby to come out because I'm past my due date already."

"Girl, just mix some castor oil in juice and drink it down then do some squats and bounce on a Pilate ball."

"You always have the remedy for everything!"

"Yep! I love my science and biology, that's why I teach it. Take care of yourself and shoot me a Facebook message or text if you have any questions."

"I will, thanks, Yo."

"No problem."

After chatting with Yolanda, I just sat in disbelief and couldn't believe I got embarrassed like that in front of my class. They rejected me to be able to collect unemployment after cutting back my hours and I had done so much for that gym; that was the thanks I got for my passion and hard work. Just like Curt, they didn't care for me or my pregnancy. The next day, the director emailed me apologizing about the pool incident, telling me how valuable I was to the program and offered me to come back to teach as many classes as I wanted until I delivered my baby but I didn't go back. The entire management staff was changing and I was too embarrassed and believed that maybe it was time for me to leave, there was no more room for growth there and I didn't want to have to get accustomed to a new director, since he was promoted to work at a new facility and was leaving. This incident was my sign, when one door closes another one opens up. Yolanda, gave me insight to another gym and I was going to come back better than ever and they'd be sorry for how they treated me. I didn't file a charge against them and just let it go. Karma came back around because I later on heard that the manager who kicked me out either got fired or just up and left to go back to whatever state he had come from and was no longer working there.

Since I was forced to stay home from the gym, I did things to try to induce labor being that I was a week past my due date. I was due July 24th and the date was August 1st and I was so through with being pregnant so I started to do some *Xtreme* training I knew would cause me to go into labor. I did speed walks, bounced on a yoga ball, deep squats, and lunges all in the summer heat. I even flipped truck tires in my parents' backyard, pouring down with sweat! I think the flipping of the tires did the trick! I felt a cramp while flipping a tire and it began to feel like contractions. My mom and I called my doctor. She said to wait until I felt the contractions two minutes apart before coming in. I ended up waiting all day, until about 1:00 a.m. That's when the contractions began to come on sharp and strong.

My father rushed me to the hospital and I texted Curt on the way to let him know it was time. We hadn't spoken in weeks and I got no response from him. I just figured I'd let him know his child was about to be born. I was dilated about three centimeters when I got there, and my initial birth plan was to go all natural, with no medicine and no epidural. That plan quickly changed because the pain was too intense, and Curt, wasn't there to help me through it. I had wanted to prove to him that I would do it without the epidural to show strength and love for him, but he wasn't there, and I wasn't going to go through with it if he didn't care.

My parent's left me at the hospital having to rush back home. We left out so fast that my mom left the oven on because she was baking and forgot to turn it off. I wasn't totally alone though because I had a cousin who happened to work on the mom-and-baby floor, and she had them take very good care of me. They gave me the biggest suite they had and made me feel really comfortable. My cousin and my aunt were in the delivery room with me. When I was finally dilated to ten centimeters and it was time to begin pushing with the contractions, Curt, walked in wearing his Air Force uniform. I was very surprised to see him there because I thought he was ignoring my texts. It just goes to show that maybe he did read them but just didn't respond. Silence is so deadly to a woman, and I believe he knew it too. He made it just in time to see his son come into the world.

After four massive and strong pushes on August 2nd at 1:06 pm, baby Michael Daniel Thomas was here. Since he was over his due date, he had a bowel movement while he was still in the womb, and they had to take him and clear his airways and examine him to make sure he could breathe. While they were working on baby Michael, my doctor began to mash down on my stomach. She pushed out the afterbirth, and it felt so disgusting! I then asked my cousin to pass me my neoprene waist belt so that I could immediately wrap it tightly around my waist to put pressure on my stomach and uterus and begin compressing down my waistline.

One of the nursing staff was looking at me like I was half crazy wondering what I was doing but I didn't care. I told her I was ready to get my figure back and she gave me a weird look like I was vain. My maternal instincts hadn't kicked in yet.

They finally handed my baby over to me, and he found where to latch on to begin feeding on his own. I did all my homework about how to get my body back, and breastfeeding was number one on the list. Even if I had failed at breastfeeding my son, I would've pumped the milk out to get the calorie burn. But it worked, and my son naturally knew how to do it, and I didn't have to do much but cuddle him. It's nature's way of giving us back our figure and also the best nutrition for babies. At that moment, I fell deeply in love with my son.

Curt was still present in the room, and so were my aunt and cousin. I wanted so badly to ask them for privacy so that I could talk to Curt, and pour out my heart to him. We hadn't spoken or seen each other for nearly two months, and I had so much to say. He just stood there watching Michael, not really saying too much. I couldn't believe I was a mom. I was trying to enjoy the moment, but at the same time, the situation wasn't ideal. The father of my child was married, and we were not together anymore.

After breastfeeding, the nurse took baby Michael to the nursery, and they prepped me to be transported to my suite. I was still numb from the epidural, and I felt so heavy. The volume of my stomach had gone down tremendously, and I had the waistband on, but it was still so big and hanging through the band. My thighs were the biggest I had ever seen them in my life, and the way my belly looked was so scary and gross. I know that many men find their women the most attractive after they have just delivered their children into the world but I felt that I looked horrible, and believed that it was very easy for Curt to ignore me and still not want to be with me.

We got to the suite, and I finally asked for privacy to speak to Curt. I also asked the nurse to bring baby Michael back. We had a long talk, and I told him how much I missed him and wanted to be with him. I asked him if we were going to get back together, and he told me he didn't think so. I began to cry, and I asked him if he could at least spend the night with me at the hospital, but he said he just wanted to be there for his son and that he had to go back to the air force base to finish off his two-week tour. I actually begged for him to stay, but he refused.

I cried, "Curt, please stay with me! I really need you, I missed you so much! I'm so sorry for the way I acted. I was just angry at you for leaving me. I love you please stay! We are soulmates!"

Curt said. "If we're soulmates then where's your band?"

"I took it off and got rid of it out of anger. I'm sorry! I was in pain baby! We are soulmates."

I had taken off my soulmate band and flushed it down the toilet when he left me. He then showed me his finger that he was still wearing his ring. He slipped it off his finger and laid it onto the tray table next to my bed.

Tears began to fall, "Please Curt! I'm sorry! I need you! Don't Go!"

He said, "I'm sorry, I have to. Take care of our son; I'll be done with my tour in a week."

I've never begged anyone for anything before, not in this way. He got up and kissed Michael, kissed me on my forehead, and then walked out.

Having his baby doesn't matter because he cares nothing for me anymore. I'm really on my own.

Bye for now,

Traci

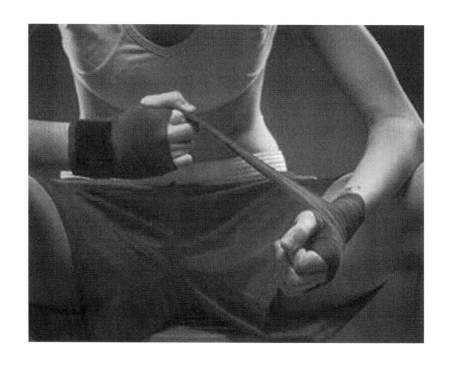

CHAPTER 12

FREEDOM: POSTPARTUM BODY BEAT DOWN

Dear Diary,

At that moment, I was alone, just me and my son. I rang the button for the nurse to come take my son back to the nursery so that I could use the bathroom and have a moment to myself to think about my next move. It was very difficult at first walking to the bathroom because the epidural was still wearing off and I felt tired and weak. I forced myself to walk without ringing the buzzer to ask for any assistance. It was like my period was on, and I had to wear these ace bandage-like disposable boy shorts with a huge period pad. It was horrible! But this comes with birthing a child. After I wiped and sprayed the water to cleanse myself, I pulled up my shorts, walked to the mirror, and opened my robe to get a better look at my body. Don't get me wrong, pregnancy is a beautiful and amazing miracle; I loved my son and he was the most amazing and beautiful sight to see but looking at my reflection, I was so disgusted and in tears at what the pregnancy did to my figure. My stomach was so big and deflated like a big beach ball; it was loosely hanging over, if I was sitting it'd be sagging over into my lap; my boobs looked massive (which I didn't mind), and the rest of me was huge, especially my hips and thighs—they were just horrible! I felt lucky that I didn't see any signs of stretch marks but I knew it was going to take a very long time, much patience, and a lot of dedication for me to get the weight off and change my shape; I was terrified thinking my skin could never tighten back up but there was no time or room for feeling depressed about it. I was free and no longer had to worry about harming a growing baby. I had to get back to work and get back to my fit figure so that I could move on with my life, be a fake trophy wife to Dr. Grey, and get over Curt.

The last weigh-in before the delivery I topped the scale at two hundred six pounds. I wasn't sure of where my weight was right after the delivery but I felt a relief from the strain I had on my back and saw that my ankles weren't as swollen anymore. For my entire pregnancy I wasn't able to work out hard and I felt that it was a prison sentence for nine months and now I was in a holding cell in the hospital. I wasn't going to wait until I got home; I wanted to pass the time by working out. Regardless of feeling so weak and numb in my legs, I grabbed onto the side of the tray table that was hovered over my bed and began to do squats using the table for support. I slowly did a hundred squats and fifty standing leg lifts on each leg. I knew that what I was doing was against doctor's orders, but I didn't care. My body didn't feel like it belonged to me and I wanted it back. I physically felt and saw a two-hundred-pound woman in the mirror, but in my mind I saw myself being one hundred forty pounds and ready to come back, I wasn't going to stop until she was back—no matter how long it took or how much it would hurt me. My nurse walked in on me in the middle of a set and I played it off as if I were just stretching and getting up to get a drink of water. I told her that I couldn't wait to get home to workout. She told me I'd better take it easy and to pace myself. Little did she know I really didn't care if I hurt myself or not, my mind was already focused and I was thinking to myself, "Get Fit or Die Trying", I wasn't going to wait.

On day two, I drank two gallons of water and ate lots of fruits and salads from the menu they gave me. I breastfed every two to three hours and kept eating plenty of fruits and veggies. I began craving protein so I ordered tuna salad with no bread with lettuce and tomato and ate it as a low carb wrap with fruit. My milk supply was very ample from all the water I was drinking. I couldn't stop having to go to the bathroom to pee, I had to be going more than I did when I'd cut down my body fat for a fitness show! I was really on to something because I knew that water helped flush out toxins released from fat cells and was also the reason my milk supply was plentiful. My boobs filled up so fast between feedings that I had to pump it out because of the pain. I began thinking that the more breast milk I produced, the more calories I could burn daily.

Again I did my hundred squats, fifty leg lifts on each leg, fifty wall push-ups, and then added a hundred hip-ups and Pilates hundreds in my bed. My doctor came in to check on my uterus and saw me doing leg lifts. She told me to stop and to get back in the bed so she could examine me and warned me of the dangers of working out too soon. She told me to relax and enjoy the hospital service and the benefits of having the nurses and aids to help me and to learn as much as I could, because when I got home, it would probably be completely different without the help. She checked my heart rate and blood pressure then asked me to remove my waistband so that she could check my uterus.

"You seriously won't take this thing off will you?"

"Nope! Gotta keep the pressure on my stomach so it will shrink faster, I did my research!"

"Breastfeeding will do that naturally. It can't be very comfortable for you to have this thing on your waist so tight, don't you feel restricted?"

"No, and I don't care."

"Well it's going to have to come off for me to check your uterus."

I took the waistband off for her and she pressed down on my loose and fat stomach, it felt so gross and mushy. It was so uncomfortable and I could feel blood leak out into my pad every time she mashed down.

"This feels so disgusting! I can feel blood coming out, it's very uncomfortable. I'm starting to feel cramps too."

"That's normal, it's called involution. You may continue to have mild contractions as your uterus shrinks back to its normal size. Breastfeeding can make them feel more intense because your baby's sucking triggers the release of the hormone oxytocin. It helps stop the bleeding and your normal cycle may not return until you stop breastfeeding."

"Wow, I learn something new every day, I actually think I remember reading about oxytocin. It's going to help my stomach shrink back faster too! Gotta love Mother Nature! The inside of me will be fine but I just hope my skin tightens back. "

Apparently I'd be bleeding for a while and then it would stop and return back to normal once I was done breastfeeding. I then asked if my skin would tighten back because it was so loose. My tummy looked and felt so squishy but she said that my muscles were unusually tight underneath all the mushiness. She also said she could tell that I kept myself in exceptionally great shape prior to having my baby because most women's abdominals tear apart during pregnancy, which makes the recovery time back longer.

I then grabbed my phone to show her a picture of me at my bikini fitness weight of one hundred forty-five pounds. She was very impressed and said she wished she had legs and abs like that. I said, "Me too!! I want them back pronto! My stomach and thighs have never been this big before!" I then asked her the big question: "Ok Doc, so how soon can I begin to workout hardcore once I get home since you claim my stomach muscles are in good shape underneath this jelly belly?" (Keep in mind that I had already been doing light workouts in the hospital) She told me that I didn't really tear during the delivery and that my core was very strong, so it all depended on me and how I felt.

She said, "I read an article about a woman in California who ran and won a full marathon six weeks after giving birth. I'm not telling you that you can go run a marathon but I can see that you are very well conditioned. You're resting heart rate is very low and threw the nurses off a bit until they learned that you're a fitness trainer and athlete. I believe you can begin when you feel ready to. Start by walking a little bit and then increase the intensity of your workouts day by day. Your body took the pregnancy pretty well so you'll be back to your normal self in no time."

That was all that I needed to hear; that was my green light. I was ready to start my intense training and workout DVDs pronto.

On day three I was ready to go home with my son. After breastfeeding for two days and drinking gallons of water and doing my workouts in my hospital suite, I was able to squeeze into my medium-sized waist cincher. I didn't weigh myself but I had to have lost over ten pounds since the delivery.

Baby Michael and I finally got home. I texted Curt to let him know we'd left the hospital—no response. How could he keep ignoring me? It just fueled me and made me more determined to get myself back. His negligence towards me was my motivation. I went ahead and told my mother what my plans were for the next few weeks and that I would need her help so that I could work out and just focus on getting my body back. Many believed that I neglected my baby, but the total opposite was true. I nurtured him every couple of hours and barely let him sleep in his crib, he slept with me all the time. I literally ate, pumped milk, slept, breastfed, worked out and did nothing else. I was staying with my parents, so I didn't have to worry about cooking, cleaning, or doing anything. All my focus was on nurturing my baby and fitness. My mother even cooked and prepared all my clean meals for me the way I asked her to, I was very fortunate.

My schedule was to wake up at seven and do my workout DVD on an empty stomach to burn more fat than carbs, then midday practice my BombshellX fitness class and/or go for stroller workouts with baby Michael so he could get fresh air, and then in the afternoon do my workout DVD again after dinner. I gave my mother my grocery list and added seafood to my vegan diet because I was craving more protein due to breastfeeding. I also planned to cut down on fruits in a couple weeks to really help me lean out.

My diet consisted of kale, avocado, pineapple, blueberries, peanut butter, tuna, tilapia, flounder, salmon, shrimp, Ezekiel bread, black rice, wild rice, apples, and red grapefruit. I ate as many fruits as I wanted and drank about two gallons of water. I began to think that if a woman's milk supply is low, it's because she isn't hydrated enough or she isn't stimulating her nipples enough (around the areola area) to activate oxytocin for the milk to come. Our bodies were made for this, yeah it feels weird at first and may be uncomfortable but you get used to it and it becomes quite a relaxing experience. Breastfeeding is what we're supposed to do, so even if a woman isn't comfortable letting her baby breastfeed directly from her nipples because of fear, she should at least pump the milk out every two hours or so and then place it in a bottle for the baby or freeze it for later, because breastfeeding is good for her body and her baby's nutrition. Even a surgically enhanced breast can yield milk for a baby if having a breast augmentation is a concern.

Years ago, I was at a fitness show and saw a beautiful new mom, who was a Figure Competitor backstage, pumping milk from her breasts. I was fascinated and engaged in conversation with her. I found out that she was eight months postpartum and she was completely ripped up with amazing muscle tone and ripped abs. She told me that she breast-fed for two months then began to take supplements to help her lean out more for her show; she continued to pump and dump her milk since it was probably filled with all the supplements and pre-workouts she was taking and she didn't want to give it to her daughter. She told me that she was the smallest she had ever been and showed me a picture of her body before her pregnancy. I then asked her were her breasts real because they looked way bigger than her before picture. She told me that they were surgically enhanced and I was so amazed that fake boobs could still produce milk. She told me being pregnant turns a woman's body into "Wonder Woman" and breastfeeding was the best natural fat burner ever. This woman won her Figure Class and everyone was blown away seeing her eight month postpartum body and holding her daughter after the show; she was in her late thirties putting many women in their twenties to shame who never even had kids before. Ever since that day, I said if I ever got pregnant I would breastfeed.

Being pregnant is the absolute best time for a woman to gain control of her body because she has the relaxin hormone present and can force her body to be smaller and have a better shape. Wearing shapewear while you have this hormone present is the best thing you can do because your body will be able to be molded into the shape you always wanted to be, and it will stay that way if you take care of yourself. Having this hormone is a gift that many women don't take advantage of. Also the hormone oxytocin has been said to help make a woman feel good emotionally and helps to fight off postpartum depression.

I was so afraid of the weight gain that I just had to do my research about it and find stories of women who bounced back fast. I began my really strenuous workouts on the fifth day after giving birth. There was a fit test on the workout DVD, I totally skipped it wanting to get right to the point, I didn't need a fit test, I just wanted my body back. I jumped right into the first workout, Plyometric Cardio Circuit. There was a lot of jumping and high-impact moves, so I had to make sure I had a heavy flow pad on because it was very hard to hold my bladder during my workouts. I literally urinated myself uncontrollably since my muscles weren't tight enough to hold back my pee. Every jumping jack and squat jump released quite a bit of urine. I began practicing Kegel exercises as well to help with this bladder problem.

The DVD pushed me as it gave me my commands, "Hit the floor! Hop Squats! Heismans! High Knees! Suicide drills! Hurdle Jumps! In and Out Abs! Switch kicks!" All these moves had to be done for an entire minute with only thirty seconds rest between supersets of different moves. It was so intense and I loved it! It was everything I expected it to be and it was kicking my butt; I was killing calories and taking all my frustrations and anger out on my fat cells.

While doing my workouts I pushed my body to the max! I rolled my ankle while doing the 1,2,3 Heisman move and fell to the floor. I saw my ankle began to swell so immediately hopped inside to get pre wrap and tape from the medical kit to wrap my ankle up. My college basketball coach would always ask us if we were hurt or injured if we fell and didn't get up right away. If we were hurt we'd get up and keep playing through pain, if we said we were injured he'd pull us out the game to see the athletic trainer to receive treatment. I wasn't going to let a minor sprained ankle stop me from my workouts so I kept pushing through the soreness. I rolled my ankles all the time when I played sports and they have never been back to one hundred percent so I always played with ankle braces. I also knew that one of the side effects from being pregnant was having the relaxin hormone so my joints were more susceptible to hypermobility. I should have expected that I'd roll my ankles with such high impact moves. My joints were loose but it didn't stop me! I wrapped both my ankles with tape, laced my sneakers up tighter, and kept up the self-imposed ass whipping.

I resumed my workout with my swollen sprained ankle, "Ski Abs! In and out! Out! In! Out! In! Attack!" I was dripping in sweat; it was all over the garage floor. It was the beginning of August and super-hot in the garage. I was burning seven hundred to over a thousand calories every workout and worked out at least three times a day. I never took a rest day and feeding my son fit between my workouts and I always fed him from my sweaty boobs! I'd use a breast wipe to cleanse my breasts and let him feed right away because I'd be in pain needing the milk to come out immediately for relief.

I pushed myself to the point of vomiting when I went for a seven mile run in ninety degree weather. This happened to be one of the hottest summers in South Carolina. I wanted to push my body way past its limits. My hair was soaked and sticking to my face and neck. Sweat was pouring down my face and body as if I had been fully submerged into a swimming pool; I threw up on about the 5th mile on the side of the road. I felt weak and dehydrated after this and my run turned into a trot, I began to cramp up, my ankles were sore and swollen up. The house seemed so far away because I'd ran all the way from the neighborhood to the mall, almost four miles away. I felt like I would collapse. Luckily my dad's sister, who lived down the street from us, saw me running on her way home from work. She brought her car to a slow speed and drove next to me. She let her window down and I saw her shaking her head at me.

She said," Traci are you crazy? It's burning up out here! And didn't you just have a baby like yesterday?"

I said," No, that was last week."

She said, "It's almost one hundred degrees today! What are you try- ing to do to yourself? Are you feeling ok?"

Breathing heavily I said," It feels good to me; I'm back in control of my body. I want this weight off me now and I'm not waiting, I don't care what any of y'all say. I don't care about the heat, its making me sweat more!"

She told me to get in the car and said," You're not looking too good, you look ghostly pale."

I said," Yea, I just threw up back there near the Prep School's foot- ball field. I ran all the way to GNC in the mall already and Guido (the owner), gave me water and said I was a beast for making it there. I prob- ably overdid it running this far while it's really hot out here, but I like the torture, it really feels good to be back in control of my body."

As much as I wanted to finish my run, I knew I already maxed myself to the *xtreme* for the day. I went ahead and got inside her cool, air-conditioned, green Jaguar. She reached into her back seat to grab something; then she handed me a room temperature bottle of water with her real estate broker logo on it and told me that she was in shock of all the weight I had lost already in just a few days.

She asked, "What happened to your stomach? It's gone! And oh my God look at your face! How much weight have you lost already? I need to be on whatever plan you're on girl!"

After chugging down the bottle of water, nearly finishing it in one swallow, I told her that I had on my sports waist trainer and had been wearing a latex one all day and sleeping in a cotton/rubber one since the delivery. I also told her about eating seafood, fruits and veggies. She reached into the back again to grab bottled water and handed it to me. By this time we were pulling up into my parent's driveway.

She dropped me off and told me," You're very blessed I ran into you young lady. I nearly had to scrape you off the side of the road! Take it easy and tell Kathy (my mother) I said hi and kiss my new nephew for me, I would come in but I have to show a property and need to pick up some paperwork from my house. I'll come back to see you guys later."

I told her thank you and she then pulled off. I limped into the house on my sore and swollen ankles to check on my son, he was still fast asleep in his bassinet. I was in great pain needing to get my milk out before getting into the shower so I grabbed my breast pump and some ice packs to ice the swelling down in my ankles while I pumped the milk from my breasts. I wrapped the ice with ace bandages around my ankles and sat down in my nursing rocking chair with my feet elevated up on the ottoman to help the swelling. I drank more water as I relaxed while I pumped my milk and began thinking of how fortunate I was that my aunt showed up to help me, I don't know how I would've made it home from that run if she wasn't there; I'd definitely took it overboard on this hot summer day. I could tell my aunt was very concerned for me. She was the one who recommended where I went for my prenatal care she has been there for me when I went through my breakup with Dr. Grey. My aunt was so excited for me when I met Curt, because he was more age appropriate for me plus he could help get her out of traffic violations if she got any! She wanted to see me happy and could see that I was in pain emotionally, she knew about the situation with Curt, and saw I was now taking my frustrations out on my body. The physical pain I was feeling felt good to me, it filled the empty void I had in my heart that was once filled with the love I had from Curt.

By day seven after giving birth, I was down by over twenty-five pounds, and I could see the outline of my abs beginning to show again and my skin magically began to tighten back. I was posting my fitness journey on my Facebook page, and my friends and family were so amazed at what I was doing. I posted a picture of my abs coming back on the 2nd week of training. After gaining over sixty pounds, my abs were almost back in world record breaking time! Not knowing the extent of my efforts to get my body back, many of my friends became motivated by me to work out as well. All of these events from my *Diary* can still be seen on my social media timeline. I know it's crazy for a woman to put her body through this type of strain and pain, but it was all worth it to me and helped me to cope with the loss of my soul mate. It's a real transformation; it really happened!

I feel like I'm getting my life back.
Traci

CHAPTER 13

STRONGER

Dear Diary,

I guess Curt found out what I was doing to myself from mutual Facebook friends and he came over to see baby Michael and probably to spy on me. The day he came over, I was in the garage sweating and doing my workout. He asked me what I was doing, and I snapped back at him, "What does it look like I'm doing? I'm busting my ass to get back into the game, and I'm going to get back with my ex and move with him to Tampa. He has plenty money and wants to take care of me and Mike. And no! I don't love him. I'm just going to be a bitch for the rest of my life and be a player and a user to get what I want. I hate men, y'all are the same idiotic low lives. Screw all of you and congratulations! You've turned me into a selfish gold-digging bitch!"

He said, "The hell you are! You aren't going anywhere and damn sure aren't taking my son away from me. Who do you think you're talking to like that?" Deep inside I finally felt the satisfaction of getting an emotional reaction and rise from him that he possibly still cared for me. I took in a deep breath of relief and silently exhaled out while smiling from ear to ear internally. I paused the DVD and led him into the house to get our son and grabbed a towel and breast wipes. We walked out to the back screened-in porch to talk. I began to feed Michael (Sorry! Like I said, I fed him from sweaty boobs daily!). He jokingly said, "Damn them tits look good! Can I have some too?" Oh my god! He was flirting with me! And it felt delightful!

I laughed and said, "No, it's only for Michael you perv." He also told me how good I was looking and that he couldn't believe how fast I dropped my weight and was ripping up. He also told me he wanted to start working out again so he could get back into shape as well.

We ended up talking about everything that went on during my pregnancy, and he told me why he was ignoring me. He knew that silence was the best answer because he didn't want to get emotional with me, especially while he was working as a state trooper and had to be focused on the road for his safety. He said he knew that I was talking to him out of anger and pregnancy hormones and didn't want to entertain me, so he left me to cool down.

"Do you understand what I went through? I was miserable without you Curt! I wanted to die. You left me to go through all these changes alone. I hated you for it! I wanted something bad to happen to you for hurting me."

Curt said, "I don't think you understand, you were not the only one going through it baby. I couldn't be seen with you anymore, my wife got a lawyer and they were watching me closely; I'm probably still being investigated. I had to end it and I knew you wouldn't leave unless I did this. It hurt me to leave you but I had to. We couldn't be seen together anymore. I'm a military man and I work for the state. I have a lot on the line to lose."

I said," I would have understood, you should have communicated better with me, I could have died, I tried to kill myself Curt!" I felt I couldn't live without you being a single mom. I just love you so much!"

He said, "I love you too. You're my soulmate baby."

I said," No, you're more than that, you're my *Twin Flame*." We kissed.

I then pushed him back and said, "Wait a minute! Where were you all those times I'd come to your house and you weren't there? It was late night and early mornings! Where were you Curt?"

"Well, I knew you'd be coming by unannounced so whenever I was off I'd drive to Summerton to stay at my folks place to get away. I also had Air Force drill sometimes. I was trying to stay away because I knew I was under investigation because of the divorce. I couldn't be seen with you, it'd give them more ammunition to use against me in court."

"Ok...Makes sense. But what about early in the morning on days I know you had to work the next day?"

"Traci, I was under a lot of stress and pressure. What do I usually do when I'm stressed? What's my outlet? You know me and should've known where to find me because you hate when I do it."

"Golfing? You were golfing?"

"Yes, I'd go early in the mornings as soon as I got off and then get a couple hours of sleep before having to sign back in to work. They guys I played with thought I was crazy for not getting any sleep but golfing was the only thing that relaxed me and took my stress away."

"I'm sorry for how I acted; I really thought you were cheating on me. Either with your wife or with someone else, I was so certain you reverted back to your old triflin' ways again. Did you notice your tires kept needing air in them? I kept letting the air out because I couldn't get your attention. I'm so sorry!"

"It's ok Traci, you were an *Angry* pregnant woman with raging hormones. You get a pass this time. I can't believe you did that to my patrol car. So was that you all those times I had to put air in my tires? I thought I had a slow leak."

I emptied air from his tires from both his personal and patrol car at least four or five times when I saw he wasn't home. "Yes, I wanted to get you to talk to me in any way I could even if it was out of anger, any type of attention would've made me feel better than none at all. I realized that I was putting you in danger by doing it to your patrol car so I started to mess with your personal car. I don't ever want to feel that way again Curt. We can probably laugh at this later on down the line."

After it was all said and done, it felt like we would be able to mend the hurt and pain that we both had. He had a lot on his plate. He almost lost his job as a state trooper because of his emotional instability. He'd just had two babies, one with his estranged wife and one with me, and then he was facing an ugly divorce process. He did have a lot to be down about, so I figured he could use the same workout program I was on to help him cope and take out his frustrations on his body in a positive way like I was doing.

"Curt I have an idea! Why don't you workout with me? I know I can't come to your place but we can still do the same workouts! I have two sets of the workout program because when I ordered it, I actually used eBay and only paid thirty dollars but it took so long to get here that I opened a dispute against the seller for taking my money. I then went ahead and paid full price to order the program through the official website to make sure I got it. Weeks later the one I ordered cheap from eBay arrived so I now have two sets of DVDs. You can have one. Let's do this baby!"

We both decided to challenge one another to do our workouts every day. We didn't do them physically together, but we made sure to check in with one another to make sure we did our workouts each day. We were posting on social media about each other's workouts and talking smack to one another online and our friends watched us. We had a bet going about who could get in the best shape the fastest.

One of my statuses said, "About to press play! I'm on my second round already today. Curt's slacking, there's no way he's going to rip up faster than me!" I tagged him.

120

He said, "That's cool, I'm doing two back to back sessions when I get off, going to lift first then do the DVD. I'm working a 12 hour shift and still going to get mine in. You can't keep up with me Traci, go get a job or something and then you can talk smack."

Our new relationship became powered by fitness; this workout was bringing us closer together again. Little by little he'd come over more to spend time with our son, and we started flirting a bit more. I would create funny memes with our son to post on social media about him losing the fitness challenge to me. All our friends and family were in on it too and placed bets on who would win. Everything that occurred is still on our social media timelines. Needless to say, we know who won the challenge! Fitness was mending our broken relationship; we were bonding again stronger than ever!

He still loves me.
Traci

48 likes

sixfootbombshell Lololol he's loosing and the bet is over on Saturday and he's trying to double up his workouts! Lol

I won the fitness challenge and the reward was love

CHAPTER 14

INSTA FAME: RIPPED ABS FOUR WEEKS POSTPARTUM

Dear Diary,

Four weeks into our fitness challenge, I had my abs back! I was down to one hundred fifty-seven pounds, and I was so motivated when I saw my abs that I pushed even harder. I changed my diet by upping my seafood intake and lessened my fruit intake. By week eight, I got down to one hundred fifty-two pounds and sixteen percent body fat. I took a selfie with my iPad, collaged it next to my nine-months-pregnant picture, and then posted it to social media. It was this picture that went viral and organically got spread all over Instagram, Twitter, and Pinterest.

Apparently a follower of my friend, Melynda (@only1_ms_stylistik, @ms.stylistik), had a massive following on Instagram, and she posted my before-and-after picture on her page. It created an uproar! There was so much negativity and people claiming that it was fake, and that it was a Photo shopped lie. She tagged me in the picture, and my social media began to blow up overnight. Out of nowhere I gained nearly ten thousand Instagram followers, and I was trying to keep up with all the comments, and mentions. I couldn't get any sleep trying to address all the negative comments that were coming in. It was overwhelming, exciting, and scary at the same time. I began to feel defeated because there was no way I could keep up with all the comments. There's so much negativity out there, and they didn't even know me or what I went through!

One woman's comment stated," Let's be real people, belly fat is the most hardest to lose. It's not impossible, but in eight weeks and with a six pack included? Hell no! It's a fake!"

One of my friends replied," keep doubting while others focus on the possible. She really worked hard for her results. Don't be a hater. Traci keep positivity over everything, you can go as far as you want!"

The woman posted," I'm not doubting, just being realistic here. I go to the gym four times a week for two hours and I am telling you that belly fat is the hardest part to loose. You can't get a six-pack in eight weeks after having a baby, it is impossible. If she said it took about six

DIARY OF AN ANGRY PREGNANT WOMAN

months or a year maybe I would believe it and say wow good job! But look at her big belly and then look at her after picture, that is impossible in only eight weeks. I won't believe that and don't want to. It's a lie and she shouldn't try to make others believe it's real because its fraud. Shame on her for using Photoshop or using an old picture of herself."

I wrote, "It's real, why are you hating? I put my body through a lot to get my results. Just because weight loss is hard for you doesn't mean it's got to be hard for me. I researched how to get my body back and I know what to eat. If you're working out four days a week for two hours a day and can't reach your goal, then you're eating something wrong. Getting a six pack starts and ends with diet, not exercise. You have to cut body fat. Hit me up if you need help but please don't discredit my hard work."

There were hundreds and thousands of comments similar to this all over different social media outlets. The only supportive people were people who knew me personally; everyone else seemed to be very skeptical about it.

My family, friends, and students at the gym who knew me personally and saw the transformation themselves tried to help by defending me on some of these negative comments as well. After word of this negativity got to the fitness expert at the local news station, I was invited on the morning news to do a live interview with my son four weeks later. The topic was about pregnancy and fitness, and I briefly explained what I did physically to get the massive weight off so quickly leaving out all the juicy details you just read in this book; they had me show my ripped abs with my thirteen-week-old baby on live TV to put the nonbelievers to rest. After the interview was over, I posted the link to the interview on my social media so that everybody could see it. I also submitted this footage along with my before-and-after picture to the production company of the people who created the workout DVD I was doing from home. The production company was so amazed with my results that they used me not once but twice on their infomercials to advertise the workout program. It was so cool and surreal to see myself on the same commercials that I saw while I was pregnant. I live in a small town and became a local fitness celebrity. Everywhere I went people would tell me they saw me on their TV. The exposure got me a lot of attention from other men and women wanting to get abs and or just lose weight period.

WACH Fox News Interview on Veterans Day 2012

Featured in 2012 and 2013 Insanity Infomercials

I got a lot of women asking me for help and I immediately began to think of how to really be able to help them do the same thing I did. After gaining all that weight and then losing it, I experienced something I had never felt before. I was once frustrated with being a personal trainer because I never really understood the struggle of weight loss. To be honest, I hated one on one personal trainings, I preferred teaching group fitness sessions where I could sweat too; I was very selfish with my time. I was actually forced into being a personal trainer at my old gym for having a lack of staff. I despised having to train men and I'd easily be frustrated if a client wouldn't lose weight or follow my nutritional advice outside of the gym.

After the experience of gaining weight myself and seeing the scale reach over two hundred pounds, I knew that I could help my clients see themselves fit. Most women can't see past the way they physically look at the current moment; it was a mental battle they were facing. I was over two hundred pounds but never accepted it to be my physical reality; I believed I could help clients reach their goals by coaching them to have the mindset to live in the future instead of living in the present moment. I wanted to help them mentally get through and knew that they needed the right, positive mind-set to do so. My passion for fitness and helping only women exclusively was ignited by my postpartum transformation.

Opportunity is knocking,
Traci

CHAPTER 15

MARRIAGE: BOMBSHELL THE BUSINESS

Dear Diary,

I have some awesome news! I was able to get hired working at a new gym called Muscle Pro Athletic Club a couple weeks after I got home from the hospital. The owners of this new gym were a cute, married Latin couple, Maria and Tony, they knew about me before I applied there! They told me they heard about me having a good reputation for teaching fun and intense high calorie burning classes. They were excited I came to them and wanted to have me instruct in their facility because I had many styles of teaching and different certifications to bring even more of a variety of classes to their establishment.

At this meeting with the new owners, Maria asked me the reason why I left my old gym. I told her about the pregnancy discrimination and how it made me feel really underappreciated as an employee and instructor who had packed out classes. I told her how I literally had lines of people outside the door at five am waiting to get a bike for my spin class, my *Zumba* class had to be moved to the basketball courts because so many women wanted to take my class and we couldn't safely fit in the group x room; over one hundred bodies sometimes. My *Pump* class ran out of equipment for everyone to participate, and my water aerobics class was always crowded. I was really a big deal at my old gym and taught fifteen to over twenty hours worth of classes per week before they began to cut back my hours because of my pregnancy, they cut back my hours at a time when I needed them the most. The owners then asked me how many days and classes did I want to teach and also asked what my pay was at my old gym.

"They paid me seventeen per class; I can fill in wherever you need me to. I'm just really excited to get back teaching again and establish a new following."

Tony said," Seventeen dollars a class! That's it? How about we double that. How does thirty-five per class sound to you?"

I said in excitement, "Oh my God really?"

Tony said," Yes, you are worth it, look what you just did! You just had a baby and look at you! You're ripped up! You're so motivating and we need that type of passion around here. We can tell you really love what you do and you live by what you preach. You are very valuable and we want to pay you what you are worth. If you were instructing here with us while you were pregnant you would have been treated like a queen! Maria and I don't have any daughters; we would have treated you as if you were one of our own. We are family here and value our employees as if they are family."

I felt so at home already, this was a family owned gym and they all worked together, mom, dad, and sons, they made me feel very welcomed and appreciated. These owners became my new gym parents and I began to learn about what it takes to run a fitness facility while working with them.

Everyone was so in shock of how soon I was back to being active and in shape able to show my rock hard abs. My passion to aid with weight loss was refueled, and I only wanted to help women. After a few weeks went by, my gym parents encouraged me to start back personal training again because the gym members wanted it.

With a fast and heavy Latin accent, Tony said, "Mira hija, if I was you, I'd have a million dollars sitting in my bank account. You are very marketable. Your face is bein' seen on those fitness infomercials all over de United States; you were on the morning news! People respect you and listen to you, you're very attractive, and you're passionate and know your stuff. I mean people would rub horse dung on their stomachs if you told them you did it to get your abs! You did an amazing thing after you had your son, If I were you I would run with it and use it to my advantage. If you were my biological daughter, you would know a thing or two about this business already and would be a millionaire. Habla con Maria, she has a Doctorate in Nutrition, and you can learn a lot from her. Don't limit yourself darling, you have a gift and can go very far. I have a few names of members who want personal training and I'm giving you precedence over the otro trainers."

"OK. Only women though, I don't like training men."

"You got it darling!"

Tony always gave me motivational talks; he was so filled with positive energy and was a big dreamer. He told me how their gym has survived for so long and how they first got their gym started in 1983, the year I was born. After the pep talk with Mr. Tony, I thought on it long and hard and then did research about businesses. I visited the business office at South Carolina State University to get a few questions answered and also for guidance. The school helped me to attain an LLC and I went ahead and formed my own training business. Many women began to reach out to me, so why not turn it into a business? I played around with different names and then decided to use the name I got while working at the sexy restaurant, *SixFootBombshell*, but I took off the 'SIX FOOT' and added *'XTREME'* to represent the intense training I put my own body through postpartum. I branded my own group fitness class and named it BombshellX which was a mixture of all of my certifications into one cardio/strength class with my own musical selections. It's really girly and women loved it!

I later became a health coach, and I was able to expand my services further than just being in the gym. I was so busy! I was spending so much time in the gym having to use my breast pump to keep an ample supply for my son at home with my mom. On top of teaching many classes, I had about fifteen to twenty gym clients in rotation daily, and then I took to having an online presence and began helping women all over the world to achieve their fitness goals with my training and coaching. I had gained a wealth of knowledge about nutrition from Tony's wife, Maria, and also being part of Team Bombshell ultimately gave me an advantage in knowing how to run my coaching business effectively online. I received the best training and preparation from this team and wanted to mimic the same style of business it used. I structured my company the same way this team structured theirs for distance training. Instead of preparing women for fitness shows, I was in the business of preparing women for life before, after, and during pregnancy with lifestyle fitness training and nutrition.

I began to get more popular on social media with more followers and clients; my online training started to take off fast. Business began to boom, and I was able to completely leave the gym and work from home to be closer with my son after six months of hard work helping women all over world. I let my gym parent's, Tony and Maria know I was ready to step out on my own and really focus on my online business. I have trouble saying goodbye but I thanked them for encouraging me to step out of my comfort zone to grow myself and giving me my start. I also told them that when I get my first million in the bank, I'd come back and make a contribution to the gym. After I left, they were blessed with being able to turn into one of the world's biggest gym franchises and have become the town's best high end and most exclusive gym.

It felt good to be on my own and everything seemed to be moving so fast after the postpartum controversy. My new found passion took all my attention off Curt, and our relationship and I had finally found peace within myself and my life. All of my energy was going into being a mother to my son and helping my women clientele to live healthier and fit lives. I was very busy and fulfilled beyond what I ever imagined and I guess my new found passion was very attractive to Curt, because he asked me to marry him soon after his divorce was finalized (his ex-wife was already remarried and moved away before his proposal to me). We immediately began to house hunt and I purchased my dream car for my business, which was a yellow Hummer SUV. I placed my *Bombshell Xtreme Fitness* logo on the truck and I called it my *Bombshell Mobile*.

Since I was just getting my business up and running, we opted for a more budget-friendly wedding. We didn't want to have a traditional, extravagant, and expensive wedding to create debt, so we invested in finding our dream home. Many young couples I know spend thousands on their wedding and then move into an apartment and rent; I've witnessed some women spend nearly five figures or more on just their dress alone! Maybe we can have another ceremony later but I didn't want to splurge on a wedding party at this time; I had business on my mind. The home we fell in love with was a beautiful and secluded country lake house with a two-story Morton building that needed much renovating but perfect to build a spacious and private personal training studio. The house also had a two car garage roomy enough to train my clients until the Morton Building gets turned into my BombshellX Studio. I could picture myself teaching Pilates classes right on the lake and it would be so peaceful and private.

After getting the house, we got the landscaping done and fixed it up to be the location for our small private wedding ceremony. The budget was fifteen hundred dollars, and the ceremony was outdoors on the lake in our new backyard. Although we had a very small budget, the location was priceless and our small wedding was breath taking and our guests didn't expect it because nobody knew that we got the house until the wedding day. It was so gorgeous and sentimental at our new home, the place we'd begin our new chapter of life together. Our wedding cake was very unique and symbolized how we met and how we got back together.

www.CakesRock.rocks Location:Austin Texas

The Cake's Theme was **Insanity**, which was the workout that mended our broken relationship. Our Cake topper was of Curt in his State Trooper Uniform with the details of his real badges. He was lifting a heavy weighted bar with me on top of it and I was handcuffed from my leg to his hand. I had on an Insanity Sport Bra and shorts with a microphone headset because I taught Insanity as a group fitness class at my new gym (the first person in the entire state of South Carolina to be certified to teach Insanity at that time). At Curt's feet was our son, Michael, who was sucking his two fingers(like he does in real life) and also the Buck deer that represented the deer wreck I had that brought us together as a couple from the very beginning when we met. It was literally an insane looking wedding cake!

The only thing that went wrong with my wedding day was that my dress wouldn't fit. I was over an hour late for my wedding because I had no backup dress. My mother had to safety pin the dress shut, and thank goodness my weave was long enough to cover up the pins. Me of all people—the trainer who trained hard to look good in her dress—couldn't get it zipped up despite having great dress fittings weeks before. I found out a couple days after the honeymoon that I was seven weeks pregnant. The reason my dress didn't fit was because I had begun to gain weight already. As excited as we were to be pregnant, it didn't last too long. I was devastated when I found out the pregnancy was ectopic and had to be terminated.

This time was very challenging for me and my business because I became very depressed again and actually had to sit out after the surgery and follow the doctor's orders for six weeks no physical activities. I had a bikini line incision that had to heal. During this downtime I actually created workouts that C-section postpartum women with limited mobility could comfortably do. I turned a setback into a comeback because I finally had the experience of actually having to wait those dreadful six weeks to become active again. Everything happens for a reason, and I feel that this ectopic pregnancy occurred so that I could experience what it felt like to have to wait six weeks after you give birth to begin working out again.

Since being married and working from home, I have met and networked with so many women all over the world. The highlight of my career was when I was contacted by a well-known celebrity for a bikini fitness plan and distance training. I was kind of star struck because she was an iconic rap artist who I listened to and have bought every album from as a child. She was so cool and down to earth; then I found out that she was a Virgo and that explained why we got along so well. At that moment, I knew I was being blessed and good karma was coming back around. I also became the official trainer for a local pageant director and her queens; I train a reality star; became a high school cheerleader conditioning trainer, and of course, I train expecting and new moms. I travel all over with my business. I'm living my dreams, and I'm so thankful for the challenging trials I had to go through in order to get to where I am today. From the success of Bombshell Xtreme, I was able to retire my husband from the highway patrol and he became a full time motivational speaker and an author. He inspired me to write my experiences into book form and I inspired him to become a certified group fitness instructor. He will help with group trainings and we will be adding a special Couple's Fitness Training to the business in the future, believing that fitness can be therapeutic to relationships, bringing couples even closer together.

Even though a situation can look and feel hopeless, you just have to keep pushing forward; I am glad that I didn't give up when everything seemed despairing for me. I'd like to continue to grow and extend my services to all those women who need help and motivation to get fit and stay fit. I am also writing my second book to help teenage girls stay focused on their dreams to become whatever they want to be. Overall wellness and fitness are my passion and I make the journey fun and easier to maintain than the old-fashioned, traditional ways. Our mottos are "Empowering Women to Be Fit for Life and Cultivating Outstanding Women Now." No matter what troubles and trials come your way, you can always overcome. You have to fight through some bad days in order to earn the best days of your life. Just when I thought I would never find love or happiness the unexpected happened (The Deer Wreck) and I am thankful that I was able to make it through all the trials that crossed my path.

I know life can be unpredictably crazy and not go exactly as we plan but we do have a certain degree of control as to what events do occur through free-will and choice. This diary shines a negative light on my character but I'm willing to share my story because I know it may help inspire someone to keep pushing forward. I'm no different from the majority of women on this planet, I wanted love and to be loved so badly. Women are built to be maternal, to love, nurture, and to be adored; I did end up finding companionship and did whatever I could to secure it. I'm very blessed to have my son, but the way in which I conceived him was very selfish and not a very wise move on my part; I know it will not be praised by many but I'm sure I'm not the first woman to do something devious like that. I learned my karmic lesson for staging my pregnancy and definitely got what I deserved.

When I reflect back on what I went through and everything I've done, I can clearly see that I had some serious self-esteem issues. It's completely normal to go through emotional times of depression and times of feeling really good but I guess my esteem wasn't considered to be healthy. It affected my relationships and ability to make good decisions. Self-love/esteem virtually affects every part of our lives and maintaining a healthy and realistic view of ourselves will make us women more resilient and better able to weather stress and setbacks in life.

A great example of a healthy self-esteem is the gorgeous plus size fashion model, Tess Munster. Her beauty platform is in contrast with the industry in which I work in but I really admire her because she knocks all of these superficial standards of what is considered beauty out of the ball park with her voluptuously short, plus size, and curvaceous figure. She is highly criticized in the fitness community for her size but her positivity and amazing spirit, not to mention her beauty, outshine all the hate she receives from critics. I believe that if I had Tess's attitude about having a better relationship with myself and my body at an earlier age, instead of looking for it externally, I probably would have been more successful earlier on in my life. Self-love could have saved me from many heart breaks and pains I went through.

Every aspect of love is the cure to pain, suffering, and hate. Women are very powerful beings because when she is in love with herself and other people around her, the positive energy that she emanates affects all those around her and there is peace. My favorite movie is called, The Fifth Element, and the love found inside of a woman is portrayed as the fifth element (the other elements are earth, fire, wind, and water) on the planet in this movie; this love actually saves the world from the destruction of evil. That being said, the next chapters contain helpful information I'd like to share about health and the well-being of the heart and spirit.

Twin Flames
Encountered 1/15/2011 (Deer Wreck)
Married 9/7/2013

CHAPTER 16

LOVE: RELATIONSHIPS & WELL BEING OF THE HEART

I recall reading a fitness article in a magazine about, Kelly Rowland (Former singer from Destiny's child), where she stated that finding your soulmate is one of the ways to stay happy, healthy, and fit. Kelly was right on with this because a meaningful and intimate connection with another person is definitely great for your emotional and spiritual well-being/heart health. Nothing in this world feels better than a true union of unconditional love between two people. I believe love is what we were created to experience as human beings. Finding true love is wealth and no money can buy it. There have been studies that show love can have healing powers and actually cure physical ailments in the body, it's truly an amazing thing that can actually save lives.

When I analyze love in my brain, I break it down and view it as physics and chemistry, it's so vast and there are many chemicals in the body that causes us to love others. Even though we don't see it with our naked eye, we can feel it and it's definitely scientific. When a man and a woman are first attracted to one another, they're driven by their sexual hormones, estrogen and testosterone. Then adrenaline and other neurotransmitters causes you to really be captivated by them before becoming totally attached. The hormone oxytocin then causes us to become devoted and loyal to our lovers and it's said to be released during sexual orgasms and when a woman breastfeeds her baby. All these chemicals greatly affect the quality of life we live as humans.

I truly believe that having a high self- esteem with a great balance of health physically, mentally, and spiritually are essential to living a higher quality, long, and healthy life. Being physically fit is great but if mentally, emotionally, and spiritually you aren't healthy, then it is just as bad as being physically unfit, there should be a good balance. If you haven't found your soulmate yet then it's a great idea to take that energy of love and put it into yourself, love yourself first, and take care of yourself physically. Every workout and every healthy meal should be the love energy given to your body in preparation for your mate. This "Self-Love" will give you a higher esteem and should stay with you forever, even after you find your special somebody.

If any of this information is new to you, I'd like to share how I learned about finding a soul mate. I grew up in a Christian family where religion played a big role in my life. Every Sunday we went to church and I participated in many activities within the church, including the children's choir and the junior usher board. I also attended a private all girl Catholic high school. Religion has been instilled in me since birth and I believe it's very necessary, especially within the youth of today, to teach them wrong from right and to indoctrinate the correct morals to live by. I am thankful for all I have learned through my schooling and the church because I have been taught great ethics. My parents and teachers did an excellent job educating and raising me. I have only come to realize in the last thirteen years of my life that I like the idea of being spiritual rather than religious and labeling myself after a denomination or a system of beliefs.

Thirteen years ago (In 2001), I began to search for answers about myself and about the world; what I discovered was much deeper and way more than what I have ever been taught through religion. The information I found out changed my life forever. It was very enlightening and exciting to find, almost like a hidden treasure!

What I discovered about myself was that there is a metaphysical energy flowing throughout my entire body. This energy is called "Life Force" energy and it flows through many energy channels (chakras) in my body and the main source flows through my central nervous system from my head to the base of my spine (the seven chakras). This energy comes from God/The Universe and is said to give me life, hence the name, "Life Force Energy". This is something that is taught to anyone who takes any form of martial arts. Every living thing (animal and plant cells) has this energy flow, not just humans. Just think about what has to be done if a heart stops beating. An electrical current has to be implemented to get it back to pumping. It's energy!

I've also learned about my astrological makeup and found out that I was much more than just my sun sign, Virgo. There are many other astrological signs that make up a person to be who/what they are, and how they deal with certain situations and function daily. We are all stimulated by different environments, religions, and upbringings but the time and place you were born make up a huge reason to why you are who/what you are. Some people are raised in cultures who praise bloodshed and the murdering of innocent life to glorify their beliefs. Even a person's physical characteristics like body composition, facial features, and hair, are formed a certain way from genetics and can also be constructed from the time and place you were born. I am a Virgo in Sun; Cancer is my Ascending, Cancer in Moon, Leo in Mars, and Leo in Venus. There are many other signs but these are the main ones I focus on and it explains to me why I love people so hard and always feel the need to help everybody. The pain and suffering on this planet are heart wrenching to me and I feel that love is the cure for it all; I do what I can to help enlighten those around me. I am an emotional caregiver and have truly come into a profession that allows me to thrive in my passion where I can help women to achieve physical, mental and emotional health through physical fitness and nutrition.

Knowledge about who/what you are can help you on your journey to ultimate love, health, and happiness. Finding out your first five signs is a great start. You need to know your time and place of birth. There are many websites you can visit to find out your Sun, Moon, Mars, Venus, and Ascending/Rising sign. Just Google or Yahoo search and it should get you all the information you need, there's tons of it. Why is this information important? I believe it is very important in finding your connection to your soulmate and/or your Twin Flame. Astrological signs play a major role in how compatible you are in relationships with other people not just romantic connections. Whenever I had college professors, or a job with a boss or superior, I always wanted to know what their sun sign was so that I could know the type of person I was dealing with and maybe be able to get along with them even better knowing kind of what made them tick; Romantic relationships are likewise, you really want to get with someone you are most compatible with and it goes way deeper than just the one-dimensional sun sign.

I am no expert in relationships, astrology, or metaphysics but I do believe that these signs play a major role in the spiritual composition of every individual soul. Every person who was born is born at a certain time and space in the cosmos. The sun moon and planets are aligned at certain degrees which make each individual's makeup and spiritual body composition very unique to that time and space; it's just like a fingerprint. Think of this for example, the human body is about seventy percent water and the planet Earth is about seventy-one water. If you really think about that, imagine how the moon influences the bodies of water on this planet. The gravitational pull causes low tide and high tide. The same gravitational influence happens to the human body. The moon is known as the "ruler of emotions" and can cause a shift in the chemical balance of elements and therefore cause an effect on the emotions in a human body. When there is a full moon it is said that people get a little crazier. Think about the term *Lunar*, it's related to *Looney* and *Lunatic* which means crazy. I'm such a Virgo and think about silly stuff like this always trying to analyze everything. I don't want to get too deep into this subject matter because that could be an entirely different book and I'm sure an expert has already written one!

The point I want to make is that really finding out whom and what you are spiritually can greatly impact the relationships you have and your destiny on this planet. A person can go through many romantic relationships in their lifetime. You can love hard and then have your heart broken over and over again. I know I've had my share of broken hearts many times and these relationships felt like Soulmate connections. I just recently discovered that one can encounter many soulmates throughout their lifetime. First of all, I don't even think I really explained what a soulmate is. Well, a soulmate is someone you feel deeply connected to and form a lifelong bond with this person. While doing research about soulmates, I found out that you are supposed to learn and grow from these types of relationships and the experience prepares you to ultimately meet your "Twin Flame". What is a twin flame? Well I've never heard of a Twin Flame until I did my research to find out more about myself. Believe it or not, it gets even better than just having a soulmate!

What I learned is that a twin flame relationship is the most powerful type of relationship that we can experience as a human being. Your twin is literally the other half of your soul, Ying and Yang energies combined. The love is unconditional and has no limit, this bond is the

"Ultimate Power Couple" and it is very intense. Once you meet this person, you become a complete and ultimate "Power Couple" that helps to enlighten the journey of other human beings on the planet.

I do believe that my husband is my twin flame. I wanted to die when we broke up during my pregnancy because I knew I would never find another connection like we had and I was pregnant with our child. I went through several loving relationships before him that were very intimate and close but none feel as strong as the bond I have with him. We were destined to meet and met at a time that was perfect for us although the circumstances were not ideal because he was legally married. We found one another when neither one of us was looking for love, I was on my way to becoming a heartbreaker and he was already one; I believe we saved one another from self-destruction.

I am not sure if Twin Flame means you have to have the same sun sign, but it worked out that way for me and my husband. We are both Virgos with matching Moon and Rising Signs. His Rising Sign and Moon both fall under Taurus while mine both fall under Cancer. We totally balance each other out, he is my equal opposite. Another thing that's kind of crazy is we both had tattoos on our bodies before we even knew each other that showed us that we were really twin flames. I have a tribal Virgo tattoo on my lower back, a Ying Yang on my upper back, and the colors of these tattoos are like fire (red and yellow). My husband had a tattoo of two bolts of lightning on his lower abs which represents our twin flame energy. These markings were placed on our bodies before years before we met!

Finding a soulmate and ultimately your twin flame is great for your emotional well-being, health, and longevity. If I never met my husband, Curt, this book would have never been written, my son would never be here alive, and I would not be helping women to change their lives. Fitness and nutrition is my passion and finding my twin flame has been the fire that fueled my passion to make my dreams come true because before I met him, I was a very selfish individual still in search of my purpose in life. Now I share my life with my new family; I'm a giver of all that I have and have been blessed to partake in shaping and molding the minds and bodies of beauty queens, celebrities, future moms to be, and new moms. I have finally arrived and now my destiny is being fulfilled as I help guide others on their path.

PREGNANCY AND FITNESS
DON'T LET YOURSELF GO MOMS!

CHAPTER 17

FIT BODY MAINTENANCE: BEFORE PREGNANCY

FIT BODY FOR LIFE

Fitness is something that you should never give up on or get comfortable with. It is a never ending cycle that should be maintained for a lifetime, just like bathing and taking care of your personal hygiene. I coach that one should not to go three full days without working out if possible and I always tell my clients never to miss a Monday workout because it gives them a great start for the week. I also like to keep workouts fun and interesting by switching up to new workout programs, routines, and classes every few weeks. More important than physically training your body, your diet is essential to maintaining your health.

Not everybody wants to be model thin or as ripped up as a fitness bikini model, but I do believe that having a fit midsection is important to maintain great health. A strong core and back are essential to support the weight of your entire body and can prevent your body from injuries, pain, and strains in the future. Your abs don't necessarily have to be visible to be strong or considered healthy. I have many clients who love their curves and don't really care if they have visible abs or not. But in case you do want to see them, it's said that abs are made in the kitchen and working out is only about twenty to thirty percent of achieving your "Dream Body" composition. It's all about body fat percentages.

Though I recommend and encourage eating a vegan or pescatarian diet, I don't deprive my clients of the foods they love. They have freedom to choose their foods and moderation is the key to success. Eating one unhealthy meal won't make you gain weight and eating one healthy meal won't make you lose weight. It's all about what you do, for about 80 percent of the time. Once you get the right balance of clean eating (healthy whole food consumption), having occasional cheat meals (high calorie and fatty foods) will actually become beneficial to your body's ability to burn fat.

CLEAN EATING

Clean eating is practiced by bodybuilders, fitness competitors, and health-conscious people alike. First of all, what is Clean Eating? Clean Eating is the consumption of foods that are whole in their natural state, free of added sugars, hydrogenated fats, trans-fats, and anything else that is basically unnatural and unnecessary for your diet. These unnecessary additives are just for flavor and are considered "Dirty" or "Cheats". Many people use clean eating as a way to lose weight and/or to maintain their fit body. If you implement this as a way of life, it can make you feel vibrant and full of energy! Follow these simple steps to start eating clean. After all, if you plan on becoming a mom or already a mom and want to be healthier the next time you have a baby, it's best to be in the best physical shape before conception to avoid those pregnancy related diseases like high blood pressure and gestational diabetes.

BASIC STEPS TO CLEAN UP YOUR DIET

—Don't wake up on a scavenger hunt for food following your taste buds to unhealthy finds. Always plan your meal ahead to take the guess work out of what you will eat for the day.

—Eat five to six small meals daily: breakfast, lunch, dinner and three to four snacks. Try to eat every two to three hours to curb hunger and promote a higher metabolism.

—Choose sprouted grains and complex carbohydrates to give you more energy and keep you feeling fuller longer. If you are a bread lover, *Ezekiel bread* is actually the best bread of choice that I like to use and I also recommend my clients to use as well. It has an amazing nutty flavor and you can find this type of bread in whole food grocery stores. They are kept in the freezer.

–If you love pastas, a great swap for starchy pasta noodles is vegetable noodles. You can shred squash, zucchini, and other veggies into noodles and create the same pasta comfort meals you and your family enjoy but without the large amount of carbohydrates. They won't know the difference unless you tell them. They can be stir fried, served raw, or boiled just like regular noodles.

–If you love pancakes and waffles, a lower carb option is mixing up your favorite protein powder with egg, and almond milk until it's the consistency of pancake or waffle batter. When I make these, it really feels like a cheat even though I get less than five grams of carbohydrates. You won't feel as bloated when you're done.

–If you like to snack on high calorie- filled, processed, non-nutritional "junk food", then I suggest getting those kinds of foods from the whole food/health stores as well. They do have healthy alternatives at these stores that taste very good like coconut milk ice cream in every flavor you can think or, healthy potato chips, and also cookies! Moderation is the key; these foods are not prohibited to my clients.

–Eat as many fruits and vegetables as you want. Try to add one serving about a handful each per meal. Fruits make great snacks because they are full of natural sugars and water that can help fight those afternoon sugar cravings.

–Eat lean meats, chicken and fish whenever possible, stay away from processed and fatty meats. This will give you much needed protein with little fat. One serving is about the size of your palm or three to four ounces if you use a food scale.

–Try to avoid foods with white flour, sugar, and sugar substitutes, saturated fats, and Trans fats.

–Give yourself a cheat day but remember not to go too crazy this day. Allow yourself a meal out with your friends or reward yourself with a special food but try not to undo all of your hard work from the week. Having a cheat meal will help to boost your metabolism.

–If you are big on social media try to follow inspirational people and fitness pages with healthy and real images (some images floating around on social media are photo shopped and unrealistic) to help keep positivity and motivation in your newsfeed. Also you can find my contact information at the end of this book to follow me on Twitter or Instagram for motivation and helpful diet and workout tips.

CHEAT MEALS

When you're eating clean and have a low carb intake, it's likely that you can get low muscle glycogen levels. This can give you a sluggish feeling during your workouts and/or less than your optimal strength. You may also find that you fatigue faster than normal and are not able to keep up with your previous performance. If this happens to you, a cheat meal or a cheat day will serve to replenish some of the stores which will give you energy to train harder during your next workouts.

Cheating gives your body an excess of calories and carbohydrates. Most times when you are eating clean your body will sense that it's starving and it will try to lower the amount of energy it needs to continue to function on a daily basis. This means that your body begins to burn less calories while it's resting if you hadn't been dieting which can make weight-loss even harder for you. When you shock your system with a high influx of calories at one time your body's metabolism will show an increase in energy and kick start your fiery fat-burning furnace into high gear once again. This will help your body to get less accustomed to running on a lower caloric level and make leaning out easier and faster for you.

Whenever I eat clean throughout the week and then have one or two cheats over the weekend I always wake up feeling tighter and looking tighter than I was the day before and it's actually pretty fun. My gym momma, from Team Bombshell, was really good at knowing what type of cheat meals each of us needed to make us look the best on the stage.

Sometimes she would have a Bombshell eat waffles or pancakes (not the healthy protein powder ones) before getting on the stage because she knew that the body needed those types of carbs at that point to achieve a certain look or sometimes she would suggest a couple spoons of peanut butter or even a spoon of olive oil. She had it down to a science, it was pretty amazing to see and I learned so much from her.

***If you are pregnant or just had a baby the following chapters will give you information on postpartum fitness tips and also my meals and workouts during pregnancy and while I breastfed.

CHAPTER 18

BOMBSHELL XTREME POSTPARTUM TIPS

IMMEDIATELY AFTER BIRTH

Unlike me, most new mothers can't even fathom exercise straight after the birth of their baby. Apart from the overall fatigue that you'll be feeling, you may still be bleeding and generally too uncomfortable to do anything more than take care of you and your baby. However, if you're like me and want to get your body back pronto, here are some ideas that you may be able to incorporate into your day if you do have some time and energy to spare on yourself.

If you're pregnancy and delivery went smooth and uncomplicated, then a mild exercise program consisting of walking, pelvic floor exercises and stretching may begin immediately after birth. Personally since I was in pretty great shape prior to pregnancy and worked out until my delivery, I was able to begin working out instantly after my delivery and then started my strenuous workouts five days postpartum…But every "Body" is different. Just listen to it. Unless you're as crazy as I was, it's advised to wait at least six weeks before starting any type of training.

If there were any complications during the pregnancy or birth, or if the baby was delivered via C-section, you should seek medical advice before starting any form exercise.

Begin training with a level of activity that is comfortable and enjoyable for you. For example if you were in bed or in the house towards the end of your pregnancy then a brisk walk around the block may be substantial enough to get your blood flowing and your muscles pumping. If, on the other hand, you were actively taking group fitness classes and going for long runs prior to giving birth or doing kick-boxing and/or cross- fit, you may still be comfortable exercising at this pre-birth level. It all depends on your fitness levels prior to giving birth and how your body coped with your delivery. As you build up endurance and confidence to train you can gradually begin to lengthen your workouts and then intensify them. Listen to your body and don't try to do too much too soon or risk causing yourself an injury like I did. If in doubt, you can always speak to your doctor about it.

WEAKENED CORE MUSCLES

It's my belief that if you begin your pregnancy with pretty strong and tight abdominals, that they will stay intact and not split apart like if they were weak. The Relaxin hormone will allow your muscles to be stretched to allow for carrying your baby. The stronger your abdominals are, the better they stay intact. If you began your pregnancy with a weaker core, it is important to slowly build up your activity levels and not to expect to return to pre pregnancy exercise levels directly after the birth. Wearing a corset postpartum can help bring the muscles back together sooner and easier.

RELAXIN HORMONE

During pregnancy the hormone relaxin is secreted by the placenta. This amazing hormone softens ligaments, cartilage and the cervix in preparation for the birth of your baby. The down side to this hormone is having loose joints and possible hypermobility that increases the risk of injury during workouts. The effects of relaxin can continue for up to six months after pregnancy. Breast feeding can also lengthen the amount of time that relaxin levels are raised in your body; this is a good thing if you really want your figure back fast. The upside is that you can use this Relaxing to your advantage! Corset/body shapewear training will help to squeeze your waistline and hips back down to pre-pregnancy size and even smaller since your body is still in its "relaxed" state. Keep in mind that your body is tissue and that it's very malleable and fairly easy to shape. Take advantage of this hormone like I did! Women should rejoice when they find out they're expecting! This is a great opportunity to gain total control of your shape, enjoy it!

CORSET TRAINING

Wearing a waist cincher will compress your core, rev up perspiration, release toxins, and help metabolize fat. The tight fit also restricts your abdomen, reducing waistline immediately and also minimizing your food intake during the day. If you feel the need to loosen it up or take it off after eating then you have eaten way too much in one sitting; meals should be smaller and more often to rev your metabolism up. They will help you lose fat and inches from your midsection even more while your breastfeed your baby. If you did nothing but corset train and breastfeed, your waistline will shrink down tremendously because of the presence of the relaxin hormone. If you have heard negative reviews about waist training, it's because there are some women who take it step too far and do "Xtreme" waist training which can result in internal injuries. Xtreme waist training is when you keep going to smaller and smaller sized cinchers that put way too much pressure on the mid-section and squeeze your intestines to the point where your body systems begin to malfunction. If you have high blood pressure it isn't wise to begin waist training because the pressure in your upper body will increase as your heart tries to pump your blood harder to adjust to the tightness of your corset and you can get a headache. Also if you have low blood pressure the tightness can cause you to feel dizzy or lightheaded and can cause pooling of the blood in your lower extremities. Cinchers should fit tight, but not to the point where you can't breathe or function normally. If you're new to this, it's advised that you seek professional help to make sure you are healthy enough to use cinchers. Also make sure to be fitted properly and don't take it overboard to the Xtreme.

BREAST FEEDING

Breast feeding should feel relaxing and not painful. If you feel pain make sure you have a good latch. You'll know you have a good latch when you see your baby's ears wiggle and should hear swallowing and no smacking noises. If your latch isn't good, you can get sore and cracked nipples. Make sure to use cleansing wipes and nipple cream to keep nipples from becoming dry or irritated. I found it easiest to use a pillow to help with support to get a great latch. Pump between feedings to keep a backup supply and pumping helps you to produce more milk and burn more calories. You can lose weight while breast-feeding but, bear in mind that during the first three months of breast feeding a woman needs approximately five hundred calories per day in addition to her usual caloric intake. However, this does depend on your activity levels and your body composition. Breast feeding and exercise are both drains on your fluid levels so make sure that you are taking in enough water to stay hydrated...at least a gallon/day is sufficient and from my experience, I believe hydration helps with the volume of your supply.

HOME EXERCISE EQUIPMENT (THIS WAS MY NESTING)

As a new mom your time can be limited and therefore very precious. I would recommend any home workout DVDs and investing in a piece of cardio equipment. I used a spin bike. Do fifteen to thirty minute sessions a day. A good time to do your work out is after a feeding if you are breastfeeding. I've had to stop midway through training to pump my milk because it can get pretty painful when it's ready to come out. Listen to your body and if you feel you can turn it up a notch go ahead.

EXERCISE DVDS

In home workout DVDs are a new mom's best friend. There are so many out there to choose from. Pick one that you know you can stick to and do it no matter what, press play every day. Even if you do other workouts, make sure you keep on schedule with your DVD workouts and I found it best to keep a journal of everything I was eating and doing. By staying consistent and on a great schedule, I actually got chosen to do infomercials for the workout DVD I was doing because I submitted my results. You can get free coaching and someone to hold you accountable for making it through your workouts if you join an online workout community.

POSTPARTUM DEPRESSION

Don't let that "postpartum depression" set in. On those days when you feel it coming on say no to it! Go for a stroller walk with your baby and catch some vitamin D from the sun, or pop in a DVD, get those endorphins flowing. You really should be very happy at this stage and not sad. The way your body appears to be is only temporary. When a woman becomes pregnant, she should rejoice at the fact that her body will be in "WONDER WOMAN" mode. She should enjoy this time knowing that she has many natural phenomena working within her body that she can use as ammunition to burn lots of fat and attain her dream physique immediately after giving birth. You have to understand that your body is naturally in the best state it can be in for rapid weight loss, faster than any time in your life. You can be smaller than you've ever been so use this time and natural window of opportunity to get yourself fitter than you were before your pregnancy. You have a faster metabolism, you have HCG, and you have the relaxin hormone. Use these natural occurrences to get your body back! Channel your energy into taking care of yourself and baby. Take it one day at a time and best regards to your weight loss and your newborn child! Motherhood is amazing!

CHAPTER 19

PREGNANCY AND POSTPARTUM DIET AND WORKOUTS

PREGNANCY MEALS & WORKOUTS

I maintained a vegan/vegetarian diet during my entire pregnancy. Here's what I ate.

GROCERY LIST

vanilla rice protein
blueberries
strawberries
cherries
grapefruit (red)
pineapple (fresh)
spinach leaves
apples
cherries
broccoli
tomatoes
wild rice or black rice and/or quinoa
spelt tortillas or gluten-free tortillas
kelp noodles

asparagus
celery
kale
mushrooms
Ezekiel bread
avocado
vegan sausage
black bean burgers
veggie burgers
(any type of meat substitutes)
trail mix
almond butter or peanut butter
Yellow Grits

MEAL 1

vanilla rice shake and frozen strawberries
or
vegan sausage, mushrooms, onions, peppers (sautéed)
Ezekiel toast with almond butter or peanut butter
fruit of choice

or
Yellow Grits with vegan sausage and fruit of choice

MEAL 2

bean burger patty
asparagus (7 spears) or broccoli
quinoa or wild or black rice
grapefruit (1/2) or fruit of choice

MEAL 3

vegan sausage, mushrooms, onions, peppers (sautéed)
kale
quinoa or black or wild rice or kelp noodles
pineapples (1 serving) and handful of blueberries

MEAL 4

bean burger or veggie burger on Ezekiel bread (1 piece)
spinach, avocado, and tomatoes on top with vegenaise and/or mustard
small apple and handful of blueberries

MEAL 5

black beans with quinoa or black or wild rice in a whole wheat or gluten-
    free wrap
broccoli
strawberries

I ate fruits whenever I was hungry and occasionally had chocolate chip
pancakes. I drank water and fresh homemade fruit juices.

WORKOUTS:

Classes I taught: spinning, water aerobics, Zumba, silver sneakers, cardio strength

Personal Workouts: yoga, treadmill walks on an incline with three-to-five-pound dumbbells, elliptical, stair climber, light free weights.

QUICK PREGNANCY SAFE IN HOME WORKOUT:

***Its best to use belly support to support your growing belly while training. I recommend using a Belly Bra from BaoBeiMaternity.com. I recommend them to my expecting clients.

For Toning:
15 Modified Jumping Jacks
15 Wall Push-Ups
15 Standing Side Leg Lifts(each leg)
15 Standing Front Leg Lifts(each leg)
Repeat 3x

For Cardio:
Get out the house and go for a brisk walk in nature while listening to your favorite tunes.
30 minutes – hour workout

***I kept my heart rate between 150 and 170 during cardio (Not recommended for all women).
***Most doctors say stay between 120- 150 depending on your level of fitness before pregnancy.

WHAT WORKOUTS NOT TO DO WHILE PREGNANT:

–No squats (unless you're trying to induce labor)
–No heavy lifting overhead
–No sports or activities that require lots of core stability or heavy contact.
–No workouts where you lay directly on your back.
–No Workouts laying on your stomach or that strain your stomach
–No workouts in heavy heated environments

***Stick to easy cardio and light weights or body weight training and you'll be fine!**

BREASTFEEDING MEALS AND WORKOUTS

I added seafood for my main protein source, breastfed every two to three hours, and ate every two to three hours. I drank 1.5 gallons of fruit-infused water per day. I corset trained for at least eight hours.

GROCERY LIST

rice protein
blueberries
strawberries
cherries
grapefruit (red)
pineapple (fresh)
spinach leaves
carrots
apples
cherries
broccoli
wild rice or black rice and/or quinoa
asparagus

celery
kale
mushrooms
Ezekiel bread
avocado
shrimp
egg
crab meat/legs
salmon
tilapia
smoked salmon
trail mix
almond butter or peanut butter

MEAL 1

protein shake
or
3 egg whites, shrimp, mushrooms, fruit of choice

MEAL 2

tilapia (3 oz.)
asparagus (7 spears) or broccoli
quinoa or wild or black rice
grapefruit (1/2) or fruit of choice

MEAL 3

grilled shrimp
spinach leaves, kale, or broccoli
carrots
pineapples (1 serving) and handful of blueberries

MEAL 4

tilapia (3 oz.)
kale or broccoli
small apple and handful of blueberries

MEAL 5

salmon (3 oz.)
asparagus (7 spears) or broccoli
quinoa or wild or black rice (1 cup cooked)
strawberries

Snack: toasted Ezekiel bread spread with avocado and smoked salmon or Ezekiel bread spread with peanut butter and strawberries

I ate tons of fruits whenever I wanted, mainly pineapples and blueberries.

Workouts: I trained with a waist cincher at least ten hours per day and did home workout DVDs, stroller workouts, dance aerobics, and strength training. My advice is to find a great DVD you can stick to and base all your workouts around it.

BOMSHELLX BED WORKOUT

25 Crunches
25 Flutter Kicks
25 Hip Ups
Pilates Hundreds
15 Back Crunches(lay on tummy and do back extensions raising torso off bed flexing the back)

Repeat 4x

CARDIO WALL SITS(YOU CAN DO THESE WITH BABY IN HAND)

20 Hip Ups
20 Crunches
10 push ups
Wall Sit for the length of your favorite song (add overhead press, punching bags, Arnold press, bicep curls, & overhead tricep extensions with or without light weights to add cardio)

Repeat 5x

FUN STROLLER WORKOUT (30–40 MIN)

Brisk walk for 5 min (warm up)
10 lunges
Brisk walk for 30 sec

10 knee lifts
Brisk walk for 30 sec
10 reverse leg lifts
Repeat 5x

***Finish with a ten-minute fast walk or jog, followed by fifty squats

It starts with Love.
When you're doing something that you would do for free you will never work another day in your life. Life is amazing once you begin to live it with passion and purpose. There's much work to be done and the journey has just begun...
Stay Tuned

Officially Mrs. Traci Danielle Thomas

"I've come to believe that each of us has a personal calling that's as unique as a fingerprint—and that the best way to succeed is to discover what you love and then offer it to others in the form of service, working hard, and also allowing the energy of the universe to lead you."

—Oprah Winfrey

BOMBSHELL XTREME TRAINING

The Bombshell Xtreme training is a multi-faceted approach to conditioning and training women.

For centuries women have been trying to keep up with the standards of beauty portrayed by society. Many of us have tried countless products, programs, and diets to keep up with these standards, face it, we are women, and women want to look and feel beautiful. The Bombshell Xtreme approach to Nutrition and Fitness is simple. It is not a fad diet or a quick plan, it's all about making a lifestyle change and learning the proper ways to nourish the body, enjoy great meals without deprivation, and being fit for a lifetime.

The Bombshell Xtreme training method is used by its Founder, Traci Thomas, who has inspired Millions, both men and women, through her unbelievable postpartum body transformation. She trains and coaches Hundreds of women all over the world. The program is nutrition/supplement based and traverses through a multitude of workouts that include in home, gym, and group fitness classes.

If you are ready to start your fitness journey, be in the best shape of your life while having fun; staying fit for life and being an inspiration to others, the first step is to contact, Bombshell Xtreme to set up your free online consultation. Meal planning, distance coaching, group fitness, and one on one training sessions are available exclusively for women. See contact information on the last page.

ABOUT THE AUTHOR

Thomas is an AFAA-certified instructor and Certified Master trainer who currently owns and runs her business, Bombshell Xtreme, LLC, which specializes in Sports Nutrition and helping to empower women to focus on their fitness goals and stay fit for life. She also inspired millions of women all over the world through her unbelievable postpartum body transformation, which landed her an interview on WACH Fox News and two fitness infomercials that air all over America and internationally. Her customized workouts consist of cardio and body weight strength training with a focus on the core and lower back. She works with celebrities, cheerleaders, and hundreds of women around the world online, in group fitness classes, and in one-on-one trainings. She specializes in pageant and postpartum fitness and is the master trainer and fitness coach for young pageant girls, ages twelve to twenty-three, competing for Miss South Carolina and Miss South Carolina Teen. Thomas is also a qualified pageant judge for her state. She maintains her own physique as an amateur Diva Bikini fitness model and competes on an international level in the WBFF (World Beauty Fitness and Fashion Federation).

BOOKINGS, QUESTIONS, OR COMMENTS?

CONTACT INFORMATION

Mailing Address: Bombshell Xtreme, LLC
P.O. Box 684
Orangeburg, SC 29116
Phone: 914-269-8053
Website: BombshellXtreme.com
Email: BombshellXFitness@gmail.com
Facebook: Facebook.com/BombshellXtreme
Instagram: @6ftbombshell_fitgoddess
Twitter: @6ftbombshell

Made in the USA
Charleston, SC
09 February 2015